Arcade in Bradley Church.

THE OLD PARISH CHURCHES
OF STAFFORDSHIRE

Mike Salter

FOLLY PUBLICATIONS

ACKNOWLEDGEMENTS

The photographs and measuring drawings in this book are the product of the author's fieldwork between 1970 and 1996. The plans are reproduced to a common scale of 1:400 except for those of the large churches at Stafford, Tamworth and Wolverhampton which are at a scale of 1:500. Old postcards and brass rubbings are reproduced from originals in the author's collection. Thanks are due to Max Barfield for providing word processor facilities, checking the text, and the loan of a camera. She also took the pictures of the pulpit at Alstonefield, the head stop at Audley, the monument at Eccleshall, Colton, Ellastone, Whitmore (opposite page) and llam font.

ABOUT THIS BOOK

This book is a revised and much extended new edition with extra plans and photographs of a 76 page book originally released in 1989 under the title The Old Parish Churches of Staffordshire and the West Midlands County. As with the other books about churches in this series (see the full list on the inside of the back cover) it concentrates on the period prior to the Industrial Revolution of the late 18th century. Most furnishings and monuments after 1770 are not mentioned, although additions and alterations to the fabric usually are, although in less detail. Churches newly founded after 1770 are not mentioned in the gazetteer, nor do they appear on the map. They are, however, listed towards the back of the book.

The book is inevitably very much a catalogue of dates and names, etc. It is intended as a field guide and for reference rather than to be read from cover to cover. Occasionally there is a comment about the setting of a church but on the whole little is said about their position or atmosphere. The amount of material given for a particular church in this book is not necessarily a true indication of how interesting or attractive the building may be. Notable features of a church or the surrounding graveyard may lie outside the scope of this book. Visit them and judge for yourself. The gazetteer features Ordnance Survey grid references (these are the two letters and six digits which appear after each place-name and dedication) and the book is intended to be used in conjunction with the O.S. 1:50,000 scale maps.

Plans redrawn from originals in the author's field notes are reproduced to a common scale of 1:400. The buildings were measured in metres and only metric scales are given. A system of hatching common to all the plans is used to denote the different periods of work. The plans should be treated with care and cross-referenced with the text since there are some things difficult to convey on small scale drawings (e.g. stones of one period being reset or reused in a later period).

ABOUT THE AUTHOR

Mike Salter is 42 and has been a professional writer since he went on the Government Enterprise Allowance Scheme for unemployed people in 1988. He is particularly interested in the planning and layout of medieval buildings and has a huge collection of plans of churches and castles he has measured during tours (mostly by bicycle and motorcycle) of England, Ireland, Scotland and Wales since 1968. Wolverhampton born and bred, Mike now lives in an old cottage beside the Malvern Hills. His other interests include walking, model railways, board games, morris dancing, folk music, and he plays a variety of percussion instruments.

West front of Whitmore Church

CONTENTS

Inside the front cover is a map of churches in the gazetteer.

INTRODUCTION

The county of Staffordshire (in this book the pre 1974 boundaries have been used) once formed part of the Saxon kingdom of Mercia which adopted Christianity in the mid 7th century, missionaries being sent from Northumbria in 653. There is evidence that about twenty five of the existing parish churches are Saxon foundations serving either parishes, colleges of canons, or monasteries. Nearly all these churches were built of stone and there were probably also a number of small chapels of ease. From 874 onwards the churches suffered severely from the ravages of the Danes, and what survived or was built during the more peaceful first half of the 11th century was mostly superseded by more substantial medieval structures. All that now remains from the Saxon era are foundations of a small nave and chancel church at Stafford, and a tall and narrow doorway, now blocked, at Ilam. Saxon crosses remain in the churchyards at Ilam, Leek and Wolverhampton, and fragments of others lie at Alstonefield, Chebsey, Checkley, Eccleshall, Penn, Rollaston, Stoke, and Swythamley. Tamworth has 12th century structures whose planning makes it likely that it had a Saxon stone built predecessor.

Much of Staffordshire was laid waste by William I after the rebellion of 1069. Consequently there is little sign of parish church construction in the county between then and the 1130s. However, much work was executed in the mid and late 12th century, and most of the buildings described in this book existed by the year 1200, although as a result of alteration, additions and rebuilding only about a third now have standing relics of the 12th century. Much of this work comprises fonts and repositioned doorways.

Most 12th century churches comprised a rectangular nave with the main entrance on the south side and sometimes a second doorway on the north, plus an almost square chancel just large enough to contain an altar and attendant clergy. Both chambers would be dimly lighted by small round-headed windows and often the corners would be externally strengthened by thin strip-like buttresses called pilasters. In Staffordshire no examples remain as complete and unaltered as the chapel at Heath in Shropshire, but there are remains of both the Norman nave and chancel at Adbaston, Chebsey, Rolleston, Stowe-by Chartley, and the Spittal chapel at Tamworth. Only the last of these is without major later additions and alterations. Several other churches have remains of Norman naves, that at Longdon being of note and retaining a fine arch into the chancel. Norman chancels were less likely to survive the later demand for more space to accommodate choirs but occasional clerical stinginess (usually the laity maintained the nave and the clergy the chancel) have led to the survivals noted above and a small example also remains at Stretton.

Foundations of Saxon church of St Bertelin, Stafford

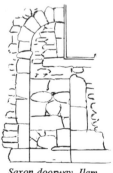

Saxon doorway, Ilam

Interior of Tutbury Priory Church

The churches of Gnosall, Lapley, Tamworth, and St Chad's at Stafford were more ambitious structures built on a cruciform plan with central towers and transepts, although all have been much altered. The last two additionally had side-aisles to the naves. The churches at Trentham and Tutbury were also cruciform with aisled naves but they and the more modest building at Lapley originally served monasteries, although parishioners used the naves for worship and took over the churches when the monasteries were dissolved. At Gnosall, Lapley, and Tamworth there are still Norman crossing arches, although the tower superstructures at the first two are now later medieval, whilst the original crossing at Tamworth no longer supports a tower. Norman towers are rare in Staffordshire parish churches. Two survive in a very altered state at Kingswinford and Swynnerton, and there is a less altered example of c1200 at Church Eaton, all being at the west end of the nave.

Rapid population growth led to a demand for more space for the congregation which was usually provided by adding aisles to the nave. Several churches have remains of Norman aisles, the arcades of round arches on round piers being more likely to survive later rebuilding than the low outer wall with its small windows. Such arcades remain at Checkley, Enville, and Pattingham.

Around the year 1200 the Gothic architectural style came into fashion, its earliest phase in Britain being known as Early English. The pointed arch gradually superseded the round arch for arcades and the heads of doorways and windows. Few new churches were built and enlargement and adorning of existing buildings was the order of the day. Fifteen churches in Staffordshire have 13th century chancels in the new style, those at Brewood, Eccleshall and Pattingham being notable. A similar number of churches have 13th century aisles or arcades surviving from former aisles of this period. Those of St Mary at Stafford, Eccleshall and Weston-on-Trent merit a mention here, but the collegiate church at Penkridge takes the prize, having both an aisled nave and an aisled chancel of this era. About a tenth of the churches in the gazetteer have a 13th century tower although in nearly every case the topmost stage is of later date, usually late medieval or Victorian. The towers at Eccleshall and Weston-on-Trent are particularly fine. Dilhorne has a rare example of a tower which is octagonal from ground level. St Peter's at Wolverhampton has the lower part of a crossing tower. Clifton Campville was once cruciform too, but without a central tower. Bradley, Colton and Drayton each have a chapel beside the chancel, and Eccleshall has a rare 13th century vestry. Coppenhall is a small nave and chancel church of the early 13th century, Ranton is a more altered version of the same, and Tatenhill has the framework of a large late 13th century nave and chancel.

Towards the end of the 13th century the simple Early English style developed into the generally more florid mature Gothic style known as Decorated. In Staffordshire this lasted almost until the end of the 14th century. The period begins with a group of large chancels of c1290-1310, that at Checkley being the finest. Bushbury and Hamstall Ridware have chancels of slightly later in the period. About fifteen churches have 14th century aisles, that at Bradley having a particularly fine arcade probably imported later from elsewhere. Norbury has an unaltered aisleless nave and chancel of c1330-45, and the small churches of Okeover and Wychnor are mostly of the same period, during which there was substantial rebuilding at the larger churches of Tamworth and Clifton Campville. The latter has a very fine west tower and spire and there are other notable 14th century towers at Alton, Audley, Kinver, Leek, Mucklestone, Pattingham, Rolleston, Uttoxeter and Wolstanton. Almost a sixth of the churches in the gazetteer have a tower of this period, whilst St Mary's at Stafford and St Peter's at Wolverhampton each have a transept remaining from it.

Although complete 15th and early 16th century churches in the Perpendicular style then in vogue are common in most English counties, there are few in Staffordshire. Only the fully aisled church with an east apse at Barton-under-Needwood, and the originally single aisled church at Horton need mentioning here. Otherwise work of this period takes the form of numerous inserted windows and the adding of towers and clerestories. A quarter of the churches described in the gazetteer have towers of c1390-1540, notable examples being at Tamworth and Brewood. At Drayton Bassett and Walsall there were SW corner towers with their lowest storeys serving as porches in front of the main south doorway. Many older towers were heightened during this period and given sets of eight pinnacles projecting from an embattled parapet with a decorative frieze below it, as at Eccleshall, Gnosall and Lapley. Betley and Rushton Spencer have timber framed churches, but in each case the outer walls were later rebuilt in stone so that only the timber arcades and roof structures now survive.

English parish churches have many furnishings, monuments and roofs of the period 1550-1700 but little structural work apart from the occasional tower, porch, chapel or repair job on some failing structure. The only later 16th century contributions of note are four towers, that at Elford being the best and still late medieval (i.e. Perpendicular) in style.

Colton Church

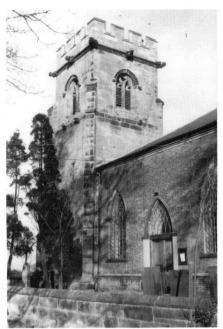

Mavesyn Ridware: 15th Century

Weston-on-Trent: 13th Century

Uttoxeter: 14th century

Ingestre: 1676

FOUR STAFFORDSHIRE CHURCH TOWERS

Twenty Staffordshire churches have work of the 17th century, including four towers of c1600-40. The unaltered and complete aisled church of the 1630s at Broughton (built as a private chapel) is a rarity. Blurton and Whitmore are more humble single-chamber churches of the same period, as is most of the church at Maer and considerable work at Checkley. Most of these works are designed in a debased form of the Perpendicular style. Kinver has a south aisle dated 1671 and much of Rushton Spencer and Seighford churches are late 17th century, bricks being the material used at the latter. Much more important than any of these, however, is a complete and unaltered church of 1676 at Ingestre. It is a Christopher Wren Classical style building of the type commonly erected in London after the fire of 1666 and Wren himself may have been associated with its construction.

More work survives in Staffordshire parish churches from the first two thirds of the 18th century than from the previous 200 years. The period starts with the tower of 1702-7 at Abbots Bromley. There are notable complete churches mostly with a west tower, aisled nave and short chancel, at Burton-on-Trent, Dudley, Stone, Stourbridge, and St John's at Wolverhampton, plus smaller churches out in the country at Bradley-in-the-Moors, Himley, Patshull, Marchington and Onecote. All have Classical style features except Stone, which is in the imitation Gothic style known as Gothick. Much of the churches of Baswich, Farewell, Forton, Fradswell, and Norton-in-the-Moors also dates from this period, during which earlier towers at Betley and Norbury were rebuilt. The Georgian style continued into the early 19th century but this book deals only with parish churches and their contents before the Industrial Revolution of the late 18th century, during and after which many new churches were erected, especially in The Potteries and The Black Country.

Between 1840 and 1914 nearly all the old parish churches in England were restored and refurnished. Some genuinely needed to be extensively rebuilt because they had been allowed to decay, or were no longer large enough to accommodate a growing congregation, but some were renovated just because it was fashionable to do so. A lucky few escaped with just minor repairs and perhaps the inconspicuous addition of a vestry or porch, but many churches lost interesting architectural features, monuments and furnishings. The items described in the gazetteers are just a fraction of the treasures that once existed in these churches.

Norton-in-the-Moors Church

Chebsey
12th Cent.

Gnosall
c1250

Mayfield
c1300

Ellastone
1588

Brewood
c1220

Clifton Campville
c1275-90

Rollaston
c1340

Rushton Spencer
1690

WINDOWS IN STAFFORDSHIRE CHURCHES

Doorways and masonry styles can help to date the different parts of old churches but usually the shape and style of the windows in the best evidence. However it should be remembered that the windows may be later insertions in an older wall or earlier openings repositioned. During the 12th century windows gradually became increased in size from the tiny round-headed windows of the Saxon and Norman periods like those at Chebsey to the long lancets with pointed heads in the chancels of c1220-50 at Brewood, Eccleshall and Pattingham. The next stage of development is the pairing of two lancets under one hoodmould as in the north transept at Gnosall. After the middle of the 13th century masons began to experiment with piercing the spandrels between the lights with circles or quatrefoils as can be seen above the trefoil-headed main lights in the north chapel off c1280 at Bradley. Quite common around the turn of the 13th and 14th centuries is Y-tracery where the mullion branches into two near the top, and intersecting tracery, which is the same idea applied to windows of three or four lights, as at Mayfield.

In the 1280s cusps and foils started to appear in the divisions. The ogival arch was adopted shortly afterwards and is used in conjunction with petal-like shapes at Okeover. The more complex designs found in some counties from the 14th century are not found in parish churches in Staffordshire, but Rollaston has an interesting window whilst those in the south aisle at High Offley show the Decorated style at its most perverse. In the Perpendicular style introduced at the end of the 14th century the mullions are carried straight upwards and generally tracery becomes just subdivisions in a relentless grid. At Madeley several windows have just simple cusped lights without tracery and in the early 16th century cusping gradually went out of fashion. By the late 16th century round arched lights, usually set in pairs under a square head, are the norm. This form still appears at Broughton as late as 1634. In the 1670s the Classical style with large undivided round-headed windows appeared at Ingestre and was almost uniformly maintained throughout the 18th century. An exception is Stone, which heralds the return of the various Gothic styles in the restorations and new buildings of the 19th century.

Jacobean pews at Alstonefield

Norman fonts are quite numerous in Staffordshire and have often survived the rebuilding of their churches in the late medieval or Victorian periods. Good examples are those at Bushbury, Ilam, and St Mary at Stafford. Fonts of the period 1200-1370 are few, but there are quite a number dating from 1370-1530, and there is another group of the Restoration period of the 1660s. Many have shields, quatrefoils and other simple motifs carved on the sides, an octagon being the commonest form.

By the time of the Reformation of the 1530s the interiors of churches that had been bare and poorly lighted in the 12th and 13th centuries had been transformed. Large new windows admitted more light despite often being filled with stained glass. Several churches retain some medieval glass, although usually only fragments and single figures as at Leigh and Trysull. Benches were provided for the congregation, surviving examples usually having poppy-heads on the ends. Clifton Campville has 14th century choir stalls with decorated miserichords or hinged heads with lips to support a chorister when standing, and there are later examples at Checkley, Enville, Penkridge and Wolverhampton. Those at Farewell are as late as the mid 16th century. The growth of choirs was one reason why chancels had become larger. Usually they had on the south side two or three stone seats called sedilia for the use of the clergy. Near the sedilia would be a piscina or basin for rinsing out and draining the vessels used in masses.

Part of a shrine remains at Ilam and a very fine 13th century sculpture of Christ at Swynnerton. Internal walls were usually whitewashed and then painted with Biblical scenes, remains of which can be seen at Alrewas, Alton, and Clifton Campville. Old doors occasionally survive, but more common is the reuse of medieval ironwork on a more recent door. Several churches have 17th or 18th century communion rails, but none of especial note. Penn has a set of 13th century tiles depicting scenes of medieval life. Church plate was usually secured in a wooden chest with iron bands and a strong lock. The 12th century example at Bobbington dug out of a single tree-trunk is noteworthy. Medieval pulpits are rare and indeed lengthy sermons only came into fashion in the 16th century when English replaced Latin as the liturgical language and at last commoners could begin to understand what was being said in the services. There is a fine stone pulpit built as part of one of the 15th century arcade pillars at Wolverhampton. There are about twenty wooden pre-19th century pulpits, mostly of the period 1600-40. Some are adorned with blank round arches, columns and other Classical features.

In the later medieval period it was normal for chancels and chapels to be divided off by screens in the form of traceried timber partitions. The screen dividing off the chancel from the nave was often surmounted by a loft reached by a staircase in a sidewall. Towards the nave the loft would have a parapet upon which was mounted a rood or crucifix, hence the terms rood-loft and rood-screen. The loft was used by musicians (important in an age when few churches could afford an organ), and by the performers of religious plays which played an important part in conveying Biblical ideas to a congregation mostly composed of people who could neither read, write nor understand Latin. No lofts now remain in Staffordshire thanks to removals by reformers in the 16th century and by restorers in the 19th century, but occasionally the access stairs remain. There are screens of c1350 at Clifton Campville, and 15th and 16th century examples at Betley, Blore, Hamstall Ridware, Lapley, Madeley, and Trysull. Horton has a tower screen of 1618.

Base of former shrine at Ilam

Pulpit at St Peter's Church, Wolverhampton

There are nine engraved brasses, about 30 incised alabaster slabs inlaid with pitch, and nearly 40 stone or alabaster effigies earlier than 1540 in the parish churches of Staffordshire. Many of the incised slabs are damaged, worn, or hidden under furniture, but there is a good collection of them at Croxall. The most noteworthy of the brasses are the ladies of c1360 at Norbury and Clifton Campville, the knights at Audley and Kinver, and the brass of 1538 reusing material of c1450 at Okeover. Hanbury has the earliest of all English alabaster effigies, of c1304, and a varied selection of monuments of all periods. There are numerous damaged effigies at Norbury. Elford, Rollaston and Stanton have unusual effigies set in recesses with the middle part of the body left solid as part of the wall. Notable amongst other effigies are those set on fine tomb chests at Elford, Leigh, Patshull, Stowe-by-Chartley, and Tamworth.

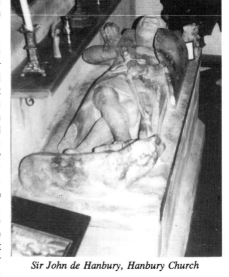

Sir John de Hanbury, Hanbury Church

Slab at Mavesyn Ridware

Tomb at Forton

Sir Edward Grey, Kinver

Effigy of Nicholas Hyde, d1526, Standon

16th century tomb at Yoxall

In Staffordshire effigies of the period 1540-1650 are more common than from the medieval period. Many of them continue the traditional medieval type tomb chest with recumbent effigies on top, as in the three at Brewood and two at Penkridge. Most of them are of alabaster and were made in a workshop at Burton-on-Trent. These tombs are usually placed against a wall and sometimes have a back panel as at Eccleshall, Ilam and Wolstanton. Ashley and Blore have huge freestanding monuments with columns supporting canopies, while at Penkridge is a two tier monument commemorating two generations of one family. Of more modest wall monuments a common type is where couples are depicted kneeling facing each other, as at Brewood, where again two generations are shown, and on the brass plate at Stone. Incised slabs continue along with a few brasses, but both are generally of poor quality after 1540.

The emphasis on effigies gradually decreased during the 17th century. At Hanbury there are two busts instead of full figures, and there are several tomb chests without effigies, as at Brewood and Draycott-in-the-Moors. A monument of 1643 at Caverswall has just an urn on a pedestal. Three dimensional monuments become rarer in the late 17th and 18th centuries when the most common type of monument is a tablet with a lengthy inscription with or without an architectural surround, urns, cherubs, or symbols of death, a profession, or claim to fame.

FURTHER READING

A Guide to Some Staffordshire Churches, Edited by D.J. Simkin, 1983.
Victoria County History of Staffordshire, several volumes.
Staffordshire, Buildings of England Series, N. Pevsner, Penguin, 1974.
The History and Antiquities of Staffordshire, 2 vols, Stebbing Shaw, 1798.
North Staffs Journal of Field Studies.
Transactions of South Staffs Archeological Society.
Transactions of Birmingham and West Midlands Archeological Society.

GAZETTEER OF STAFFORDSHIRE CHURCHES

ABBOTS BROMLEY *St Nicholas* SK 079246

The four bay arcades with hexagonal pillars and the north aisle north wall with its doorway and a window with intersecting tracery are of c1300. The aisle west wall and the classically styled west tower with pilaster buttresses and a top balustrade with urns were built in 1702-7, the medieval tower having fallen in 1688. The font is also of that period. The south aisle and the whole of the east end are of 1852-5. On the north wall is a small worn brass depicting John Draycote, d1463, in civilian dress. Of greater interest are the very ancient reindeer horns hung on the walls in the north chapel. They are used every September for the celebrated custom of the Abbots Bromley Horn Dance.

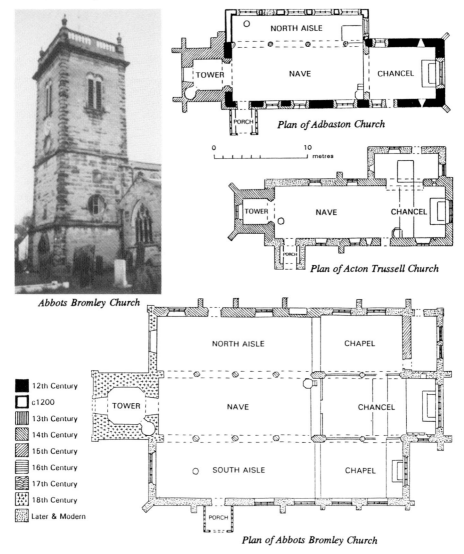

Abbots Bromley Church

Plan of Adbaston Church

Plan of Acton Trussell Church

0   10 metres

■ 12th Century
□ c1200
▥ 13th Century
▨ 14th Century
▧ 15th Century
▤ 16th Century
▦ 17th Century
▨ 18th Century
▨ Later & Modern

Plan of Abbots Bromley Church

Acton Trussell Church

ACTON TRUSSELL   *St James*   SJ 937175

This small church was originally a chapel-of ease to Baswich and only attained parochial status after the Reformation, when the original chapel lying on the north side was probably destroyed. The eastern two thirds of the single chamber are 14th century, and the western part was rebuilt in the 1860s when the porch and the existing north chapel were added. A north aisle was contemplated but not built. The tower is of c1300, but the parapet and pinnacles are likely to be of 1562, the date that appears over the west window. Under the tower is a damaged old font. There are fragments of old glass in the north chapel (now a vestry) and the east window. An architectural tablet commemorates Richard Neville, d1728.

ADBASTON   *St Michael*   SJ 763279

The nave and chancel are both Norman and of the same width. In the chancel are two original windows, plus others of the 14th and 15th centuries. The narrow north aisle was added at the end of the 12th century. It has an arcade of three round arches, now supported on 15th century octagonal pillars. The aisle windows and the west tower with eight pinnacles and a frieze below the battlements are also 15th century. The nave south windows are probably of the 14th century. Inside is a mid 15th century incised slab.

Adbaston Church

ALDRIDGE *St Mary* SK 061007

The Norman nave was given a longer new chancel c1200. A two bay north chapel was added soon after and then later extended to create a north aisle. A south aisle and west tower were added in the 14th century. Most of the building, except for the tower, was rebuilt in 1852-3, and a new vestry was added in the 1970s. Inside are an effigy of a 14th century priest and a tablet to Mrs Leigh, d1711.

ALREWAS *All Saints* SK 167153

The west tower, the three bay aisles, and a former chapel now serving as the vestry are all 14th century. Earlier are the reset doorways of c1170-80 and c1200 in the north aisle and the tower west wall respectively, and the fine 13th century chancel with lancet windows plus a low-side window in the north wall and a piscina and three sedilia on the south side. The 14th century south arcade appears to have been heightened in the 16th century when the aisle and chancel were given upper windows. The north arcade and the north aisle end walls were renewed in 1891, and the south porch was then added. On the chancel north wall is a poorly preserved 15th century mural of a Bishop and an acolyte. The church has a 15th century font with four heads on the base, two traceried medieval bench ends, two chests probably dating from the 14th century, a 17th century communion rail now transferred into the north aisle, and a pulpit of 1639.

Pulpit at Alstonefield

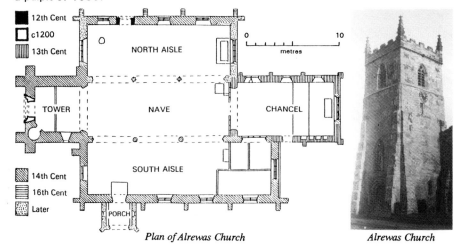

12th Cent
c1200
13th Cent
14th Cent
16th Cent
Later

NORTH AISLE

TOWER

NAVE

CHANCEL

SOUTH AISLE

PORCH

0 ____ 10
metres

Plan of Alrewas Church

Alrewas Church

Alstonefield Church

ALSTONEFIELD   *St Peter*   SK 133553

The chancel arch with an order of columns and scallop capitals and the plain reset south doorway are relics of the 12th century church. The 14th century chancel was rebuilt in 1590, the year that appears on it, and again in the 19th century. The 13th century south aisle has one original lancet but the other windows and the south porch are 14th century, and the east wall is Victorian. The west tower, the four bay arcades, and the clerestory and north aisle, both with diaper work) are of the 15th and 16th centuries. The south aisle west arch is of a peculiar shape. The north windows contain old glass, and there are Saxon fragments with interlace ornament in the porch, tower, and north aisle. Within the church is much old woodwork including a two decker pulpit of 1637, the Cotton family pew, the box pews, the lectern, the screen at the west end of the south aisle, and the communion rail.

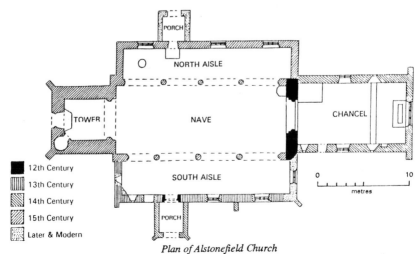

Plan of Alstonefield Church

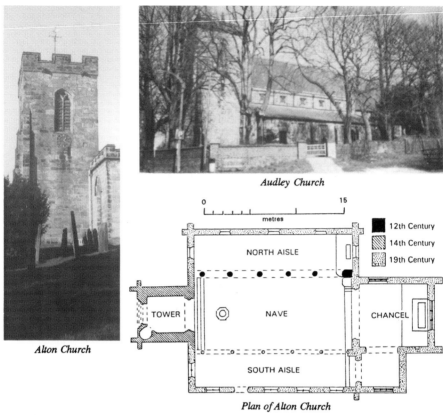

Audley Church

Alton Church

Plan of Alton Church

12th Century
14th Century
19th Century

TOWER

NORTH AISLE

NAVE

CHANCEL

SOUTH AISLE

0   15
metres

ALTON   *St Peter*   SK 073423

Most of the nave and aisles were rebuilt in 1839 and the chancel and vestry are of 1884-5. The tall west tower is 14th century and the much restored north arcade is Norman. It was shortened to five bays from six when the tower was built and has above it some traces of a 14th century wall painting of The Three Quick and The Three Dead. The font decorated with tracery and shields is 15th century.

ARMITAGE   *St John the Baptist*   SK 077165

The church lies on a bluff above the River Trent. It has a short west tower of 1632 but is otherwise a neo-Norman building of 1844. Prior to then it had a 14th century chancel and a 13th century north aisle with triple east lancets. Relics of the original Norman church are fragments of the south doorway now incorporated in the churchyard cross, and the font with pairs of crude figures under arches.

ASHLEY   *St John The Baptist*   SJ 763365

The west tower engaged by the aisles dates from c1600 but the rest of the church and most of the monuments within it are of the 1860s and later. However there is a huge monument with columns, obelisks, and recumbent effigies of Sir Gilbert Gerard, d1592, and his wife d1608.

Head stop at Audley

Ashley Church

AUDLEY   *St James*   SJ 799509

The chancel is a fine 14th century structure with ogival headed sedilia and piscina. In a recess in the north wall is an effigy of Sir John Delves, and there is a large brass to Sir Thomas de Audley, d1385, both being shown in armour. The west tower is also of their era. The aisles with five bay arcades are 15th century, but most of the aisle windows, the clerestory, and the chancel east window, date from the time of Scott's restoration of the church in 1846.

BARLASTON   *St John*   SJ 894392

The west tower is probably 15th century. The church itself is of 1886-8 by Charles Lynam. The large NW vestry was added in 1969.

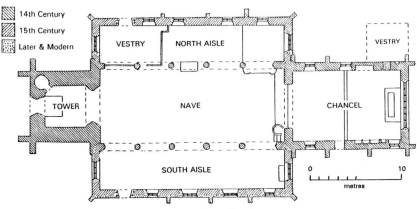

Plan of Audley Church

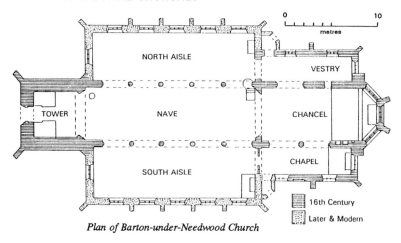

Plan of Barton-under-Needwood Church

BARTON-UNDER-NEEDWOOD   *St James*   SK 188186

The church ranked only as a chapel-of-ease to Tatenhill until 1881. The aisles were rebuilt wider in the 1860s but otherwise the whole church is as built by Dr John Taylor, whose initials and the date 1517 appear on the south wall of the west tower. Dr Taylor served Henry VIII as his chaplain, became Master of The Rolls in 1527, and led embassies to France in 1526 and 1531-3. He died in 1534. His church has five bay arcades and a chancel with a two bay south chapel, a pair of north vestries, and a polygonal east apse. The arch now filled by the organ on the north side was probably intended to take Taylor's tomb. An original 16th century Crucifixion survives amongst other stained glass of the 1860s in the east window. The communion rail is of c1700.

Barton-under-Needwood Church

Baswich Church

BASWICH   *Holy Trinity*   SJ 944224

The church has a 15th century west tower and a Norman chancel arch. Of a 14th century nave without aisles there survive the four corners with diagonal buttresses. Otherwise the nave and chancel are brick structures of 1740, and the south doorway has intermittent rustication typical of that period. Also of that era are the altar rails and the three decker pulpit, and there are arms of George III. The chancel was much changed in appearance in 1968 when transepts were added on either side of it to give more space during communion, and there are vestries of the same date. There are or were in the chancel several 18th and 19th century tablets to the Chetwynd family and an altar tomb to Brian Fowler, d1587, and his wife Joan.

BEDNALL   *All Saints*

SJ 954178

The existing building designed by H Ward is of 1846, with a porch tower added in 1873. Bednall was a chapelry of Baswich parish in the 12th century and until 1846 there was on this site a chapel with a Norman nave having several original windows and a fine north doorway. The south doorway was dated 1707, and the chancel was 14th century, with a priest's doorway and low-side window on the south side and diagonal buttresses.

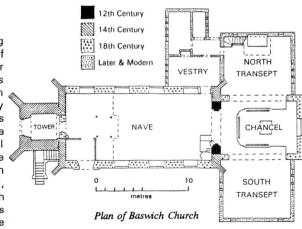

12th Century
14th Century
18th Century
Later & Modern

VESTRY

NORTH TRANSEPT

TOWER

NAVE

CHANCEL

0   10
metres

SOUTH TRANSEPT

Plan of Baswich Church

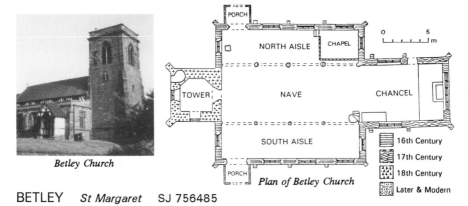

Betley Church

Plan of Betley Church

PORCH

NORTH AISLE | CHAPEL

TOWER | NAVE | CHANCEL

SOUTH AISLE

PORCH

0   5
└─┴─┴─┴─┴─┘ m

16th Century
17th Century
18th Century
Later & Modern

BETLEY   *St Margaret*   SJ 756485

Although the aisle windows and the clerestory are Victorian the wooden arcade piers with arched braces instead of proper arches between them may go back to c1300 when the church was a timber framed building. The nave roof, the screen in the north aisle, and probably the aisle outer walls, are late medieval. The chancel was rebuilt probably at the expense of Ralph Egerton, d1610, and contains the kneeling effigies of him and his wife. The pulpit is also of that period. The present tower was built in 1711 to replace an older one that had recently collapsed.

BIDDULPH   *St Lawrence*   SJ 890590

The church was rebuilt in 1833 by Thomas Trubshaw and the only ancient features are the 15th century north-west tower, the tomb chest below it to Sir William Bowyer, d1640, and his wife, and the series of eight 13th century slabs mounted outside the church which are incised with crosses and swords.

BILSTON   *St Leonard*   SO 950976

Nothing remains of the medieval church. The font dates from 1673 and the church itself was rebuilt in 1825-6 to a classical design by Francis Goodwin. The rendering and the added chancel are of 1883-93.

BLITHFIELD   *St Leonard*   SK 045240

The church lies close to the hall, far from the village it serves. The nave and aisles with four bay arcades are late 13th century but the windows in the aisles are early 14th century and the clerestory is 15th century. The ogee-headed piscina in the chancel is likely to be of c1325. The chancel windows containing fragments of old glass look more like c1300 than 1325, but are perhaps a case of conservatism. The work must have been paid for by the priest whose effigy lies in a recess in the outer wall. The tower has a 14th century lower stage but the upper part is later and may be associated with the glass of c1525 set in the west window which depicts Sir Lewis Bagot and his wives. The polygonal Bagot mortuary chapel north of the chancel was built in 1829-30, and the south porch is of 1860. Near the entrance is a Norman pillar piscina. There are incised slabs to Lewis Bagot, d1534, Thomas Bagot, d1541, and Francis Aston, d1593, and their wives. Other monuments include recumbent effigies of Sir Richard Bagot, d1596, and his wife, a cartouche to Hervey Bagot, d1655, aged thirteen, and several other 17th and 18th century tablets of which the best is that by William Stanton to Lady Bagot, d1695.

Blore Church

BLORE   *St Bartholomew*   SK 137493

The nave masonry may be Norman, and the west tower and chancel are 14th century. Of the 15th century are the north aisle with a two bay arcade, the fine roofs, the font, and the brasses depicting William Basset, d1496, and his wife. Additions of the 16th century are the north chapel and its screen, plus the south porch. Almost filling the chapel is a large monument with recumbent effigies of William Basset, d1601, and his wife, d1640, and his son-in-law, d1616. Also of the early 17th century are the windows, panelling, stalls, and communion rail in the chancel, and the pulpit and benches in the nave.

BLURTON   *St Bartholomew*   SJ 899419

This small church of 1626 with windows of three lights with transoms was altered and enlarged by Charles Lynam in 1867.

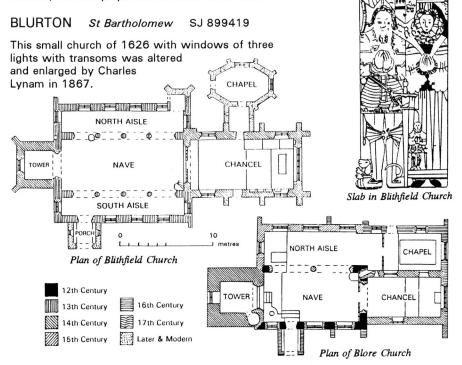

CHAPEL

NORTH AISLE

TOWER   NAVE   CHANCEL

SOUTH AISLE

PORCH
0 — 10 metres

Plan of Blithfield Church

Slab in Blithfield Church

◼ 12th Century
▥ 13th Century   ▤ 16th Century
▧ 14th Century   ▨ 17th Century
▨ 15th Century   ▦ Later & Modern

NORTH AISLE   CHAPEL

TOWER   NAVE   CHANCEL

Plan of Blore Church

BLYMHILL   *St Mary*

SJ 808123

The church was heavily restored by Street in 1856-9 when the north aisle was added. A pair of tomb slabs now in the chancel floor were found when the nave north wall was demolished and replaced by an arcade. The three bay south arcade is 13th century, but what remains of medieval work in the aisle outer wall is 14th century, the same period as the chancel, which has an external tomb recess on the south side. The thinly walled west tower of c1300 has late 15th or early 16th century battlements. It had a west doorway in 1797. There is an old oak chest.

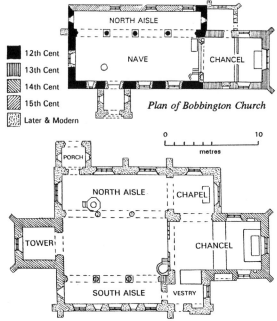

12th Cent
13th Cent
14th Cent
15th Cent
Later & Modern

Plan of Bobbington Church

0   10
metres

Plan of Blymhill Church

BOBBINGTON   *Holy Cross*   SO 808906

This is a small church with a Victorian porch-tower on the south side. The four bay arcade with round pillars and scalloped capitals is mid 12th century and the nave masonry may be slightly earlier, say c1135. Norman windows survive in the end walls of the aisle but the north wall was rebuilt in the 14th century. The font is 14th or 15th century, and there is a 13th century effigy of a man holding a shield lying in the porch. There is also a cartouche to Thomas Dickins, 1701. The chest hollowed out of a single trunk may be as old as the 12th century.

Blymhill Church

Norman font at Bradley

BRADLEY   *St Mary and All Angels*   SJ 880180

The chancel masonry with clasping east buttresses and parts of the tower are early 13th century. The north chapel is mostly of c1270-80 with typical windows of that period, although the two bay arcade between it and the chancel is probably later, whilst the form of the arch between the chapel and the north aisle looks Norman and suggests that both aisle and chapel existed by 1200. In its present form the north aisle is a mixture of 13th and 14th century work. In the 16th century the nave was given an impressive new south wall with large and lofty transomed windows and a doorway set in a blank arch. At the same time a new three bay north arcade was erected from 14th century material thought to have been brought here from a recently dissolved friary at Stafford.

One south window contains some old glass. The font, decorated with stars, billets, fretwork, a cable, and Greek key, is Norman, and reused Norman stones appear in the south wall and tower. There is a monument with kneeling figures of Thomas Browne, d1633, and his wife, and in the chapel are 18th century tablets to the Cottons of Littywood. There is also a 13th century coffin lid. On the nave east wall and in the north chapel are traces of 16th century painted texts.

BRADLEY-IN-THE-MOORS

St Leonard   SK 059414

This is an unaltered church of 1750 comprising a west tower, nave, and chancel. It has arched windows and there are lunettes over the doorways.

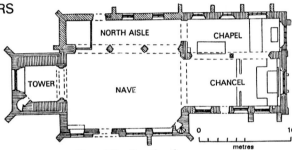

Plan of Bradley Church

Bradley Church

BREWOOD   *St Mary and St Chad*   SJ 884086

The church owes its spaciousness to the patronage of the Bishops of Lichfield who had a manor house at Brewood. The 13th century chancel has six original lancets in each side wall but the east wall was rebuilt in brick with a Venetian window in the 18th century, and then rebuilt again closer to its original form in 1879. The five bay arcades are probably 14th century, but if so were heightened in the 16th century. The aisles were originally roofed with a series of cross-gables and such were reinstated on the south side by G E Street in 1878-80. A second arcade was then inserted to create a narrow outer south aisle. At the turn of the 15th and 16th centuries a large new tower with a recessed spire was added at the west end, the series of gabled 14th century windows in the north aisle outer wall were made up into a higher wall supporting a more normal lean-to roof, an almost flat roof was provided over the nave, and a new font was provided. Two porches are mentioned in an account of repairs executed in 1665 which suggests that the south porch (probably built in the 16th century) was wooden framed, whilst the north porch was of stone. These entrances were closed in the 1770s and the porches demolished, since when the entrance has been through the base of the tower. At that period a single roof covered both the nave and aisles in one span.

In the chancel are four impressive tomb chests of members of the Giffard family of Chillington Hall. The earliest is that of Sir John, d1556, on the south side with effigies of him and his two wives. On the sides are the figures of many children, thirteen of which evidently died young as they are shown as babies in swaddling clothes. Beside is an arcaded tomb without effigies of Sir Walter, d1632, and his wife. On the north side are effigies of Sir Thomas, d1560, with two wives, and John, d1613. Other monuments include an incised slab to Richard Lane, d1518, and his wife, and kneeling figures of Matthew Moreton, d1669, and his wife and family.

Giffard tomb, Brewood   *Moreton family, Brewood*

Giffard tomb, Brewood

Brewood Church

BRIERLEY HILL   *St Michael*   SO 916868

The brick nave with two tiers of windows dates from 1765. The chancel is of 1873-88, and the west tower was rebuilt in 1900.

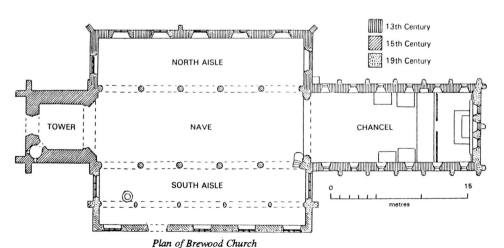

Plan of Brewood Church

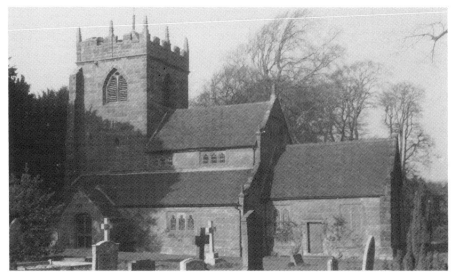

Broughton Church

BROUGHTON   *St Peter*   SJ 766337

Thomas Broughton erected this building in 1630-4 as a private chapel, and it only became a parish church in 1711. It has a short nave with two bay arcades to aisles which embrace the west tower, a south porch and a west tower. All the windows are straight headed with round arched lights. Inside are high box pews, a Georgian communion rail, and several 17th and 18th century tablets. The 15th century glass in the east window may be a relic of a previous chapel on this site.

BURSLEM   *St John the Baptist*   SJ 869895

This building, first mentioned in 1297, ranked as a chapel-of-ease to Stoke-on-Trent until 1809. It has a brick nave of 1717 with a diagonally buttressed 16th century west tower flanked by vestries, and an east apse of 1788 with a Venetian window on the curve. Prior to 1717 the nave was timber framed. There is a modern tablet which commemorates 15th to 17th century members of the Adams family and in the churchyard is a medieval coffin from Hulton Abbey.

BURTON-ON-TRENT   *St Modwen*   SK 251227

Only a 15th century font with arches and tracery patterns remains from the large cruciform medieval church which until the 1530s served both a Benedictine abbey and the town. During the Civil War the church was wrecked when gunpowder stored in it exploded. A new church was built in 1719-26 to a design by the Smiths who also were responsible for a very similar church at Whitchurch in Shropshire. The Burton church has a high west tower, a nave and aisles with big Tuscan columns and galleries, and an east apse. The interior was remodelled in 1889 but the chandelier and communion rail are of both of c1725 and the organ case is of 1771.

BURTON-ON-TRENT   *St Peter*   SK 869895

Within the church of 1880-1, designed by Evans & Jolly, is an incised slab of 1497.

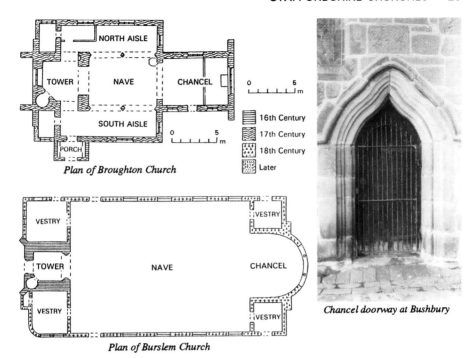

NORTH AISLE

TOWER | NAVE | CHANCEL

0   5
m

SOUTH AISLE

0   5
m

PORCH

16th Century
17th Century
18th Century
Later

Plan of Broughton Church

VESTRY

VESTRY

TOWER | NAVE | CHANCEL

VESTRY

VESTRY

Plan of Burslem Church

Chancel doorway at Bushbury

Burslem Church

Bushbury Church

BUSHBURY   *St Mary*   SJ 925025

The priest whose defaced effigy lies in a fine 14th century Easter Sepulchre on the north side of the chancel presumably sponsored the building of that part of the church. There are ogee-headed sedilia on the south side and one of the windows has some original glass. Most of the large aisled nave with five bay arcades was rebuilt in the 19th century when the 15th century south aisle was doubled in width. Until then there were Norman doorways on both the south and north sides. The latter (the simpler and plainer of the two) survives in a refaced condition. The west tower is 16th century. The tiny 20th century Staveley-Hill family chapel has a unique position projecting diagonally from the south-east corner of the south aisle.

BUTTERTON   *St Bartholomew*   SK 076566

In the church of 1871-3 and 1879 is a 14th century font with representations of windows with intersecting tracery.

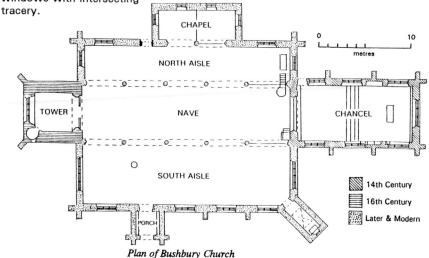

Plan of Bushbury Church

CALTON   *St Mary*   SK 106501

The church was rebuilt in 1762 and restored in 1875. Within it is a communion rail with foliage panels of c1670.

CANNOCK   *St Luke*   SJ 982101

The north aisle has some 12th or 13th century masonry. At that time the building was a chapel-of-ease to Penkridge, but it was recognised as a parish church by the Bishop in 1293. The arcades are 14th century and the west tower (rebuilt in the 16th century) and north chapel were also originally of that period. Most of the south aisle is of 1753, and a fine classical style south doorway of that period was removed when the south chapel and porch were added in 1956. The church was extended eastward in 1878-82, the period of the eastern two bays of the nave and aisles, the chancel, and the vestry. There is an old chest. The tablet to Mary Warying, d1613, had lost its figure of her by 1836.

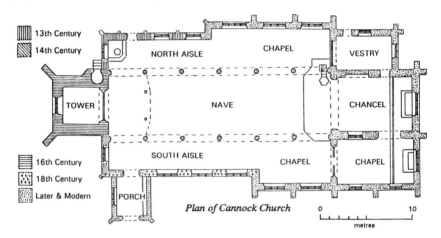

Plan of Cannock Church

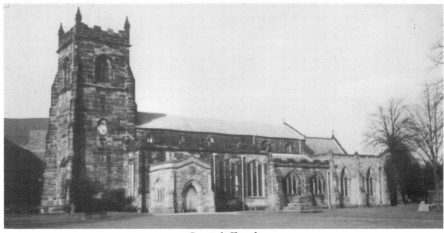

Cannock Church

CASTLECHURCH   *St Mary*   SJ 906222

This church served the lords of Stafford Castle high on a hill above it and was dedicated to St Lawrence from at least 1742 until 1898. Except for a diagonally buttressed 15th century west tower and a Saxon or Norman coffin lid with abstract decoration, the building is of 1844, with a north aisle added in 1898. Prior to 1844 the nave north wall had a Norman doorway and window, whilst the south wall was an 18th century brick structure. A worn shield on the tower west window is said to have born arms commemorating a marriage between the Staffords and Nevilles in 1424, whilst the tower top may be of the period of the sundial dated 1624.

CAULDON   *St Mary and St Laurence*   SK 078495

The west tower, nave, north arcade with square piers, and parts of the chancel date from 1781-4. However, most of the chancel masonry is earlier, and is perhaps medieval. The porch was added in 1885 and the north aisle was rebuilt in 1926.

CAVERSWALL   *St Peter*   SJ 951428

The chancel dates from c1200 and has one original lancet window on the north side. The 13th century arcades were originally of six bays but the west bay was later truncated, either in the 14th century when part of the north aisle was rebuilt, or in the 15th century when the west tower was built. The clerestory, parts of the outer walls of each aisle, and two chancel windows are probably early 17th century. In 1962 part of a 12th century tympanum was found reset in a north aisle window. The earliest of several monuments and tablets is that to George Cradock, d1642, who built substantial parts of the adjacent Caverswall Castle.

CHAPEL CHORLTON   *St Lawrence*   SJ 813377

All that survived the rebuilding by James Trubshaw in 1826-7 was the Jacobean pulpit and some of the internal masonry of the west tower.

Caverswall Church

CHEBSEY   *All Saints*   SJ 860286

The nave and chancel are both structurally Norman, each having some remains of an original north window, and the nave also having pilaster buttresses on the west corners and a Late Norman south doorway. The narrow south aisle with a four bay arcade and the chancel arch are 13th century. Several windows in the nave and aisle are 14th century, the west tower, the chancel windows, and probably the nave roof, are 15th century, and the porch is of 1707. Only the vestry is Victorian. The communion rail with twisted balusters is of 1682, the font is dated 1704, and there is a 13th century stone coffin with a finely carved lid. In the churchyard are remains of a Saxon cross-shaft.

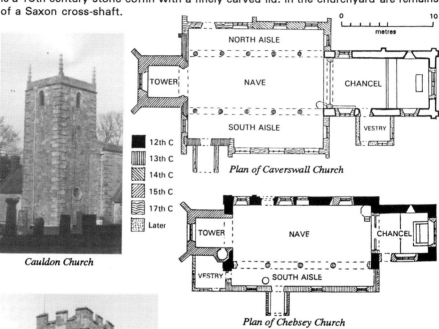

12th C
13th C
14th C
15th C
17th C
Later

Plan of Caverswall Church

Plan of Chebsey Church

Cauldon Church

Castlechurch Church

Chebsey Church

Checkley Church

CHECKLEY   *St Mary*   SK 028379

The north arcade is early 13th century. The late 12th century south arcade is unusually lofty for its period but was probably raised in the 17th century when the embattled clerestory and porch were added and the aisle outer walls rebuilt. The south doorway is a fine specimen of c1300 as is the chancel which has windows with intersecting tracery with rosettes at the points of intersection and some original glass. The tower looks 14th and 15th century but could be of the time of the 17th century rebuilding, whilst the flat buttress at the NE corner is probably a relic of the original Norman nave. The Norman font has various carvings including a depiction of a donkey. In the chancel are stalls dating from c1535 and effigies of a cross-legged early 14th century knight and of Godfrey Foljambe, d1560, and his wife. Two fragments of a Saxon cross lie in the churchyard to the south of the porch.

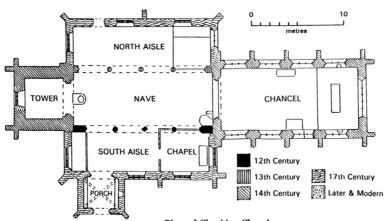

Plan of Checkley Church

CHEDDLETON   *St Edward*   SJ 971524

This church ranked as a chapel-of-ease to Leek until 1450. The lower part of the west tower, the north aisle, and the fine chancel with ogee-headed sedilia and a piscina with ballflower in the mouldings are all 14th century, but the north arcade goes back to the 13th century. The south aisle was added in the 15th century but its windows are Victorian, as are the chancel east window and the vestry. The top stage of the tower is of the 1570s and the south porch was added about the same period. Set in the middle of the reredos is a 15th century Flemish representation of the Decent from the Cross.

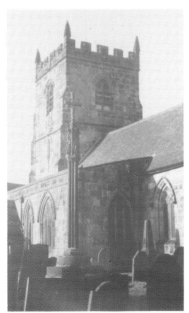

Saxon cross fragments, Checkley

Plan of Cheddleton Church

VESTRY

NORTH AISLE

TOWER

NAVE

CHANCEL

SOUTH AISLE

PORCH

14th Century
15th Century
16th Century
Later & Modern

0   10
metres

Cheddleton Church   *Chancel at Cheddleton*

CHURCH EATON   *St Editha*   SJ 848176

The west tower with its small west windows and clasping buttresses is late 12th century, and the recessed spire is 15th century. Parts of the thin south wall of the nave may also be Norman, and there is a broken font of that period decorated with billets. frets and sunken stars. The five bay north arcade is 13th century, but the aisle itself was rebuilt in the late 14th century and later extended eastward to create the Crockett chapel, beyond which is a small vestry of c1600. The chancel east wall is entirely filled by a 16th century window of seven lights. The large vestry and south porch are of 1889. The nave roof formerly had a beam dated 1597 with initials of Walter Giffard. The chapel has many memorials to the Crockett family.

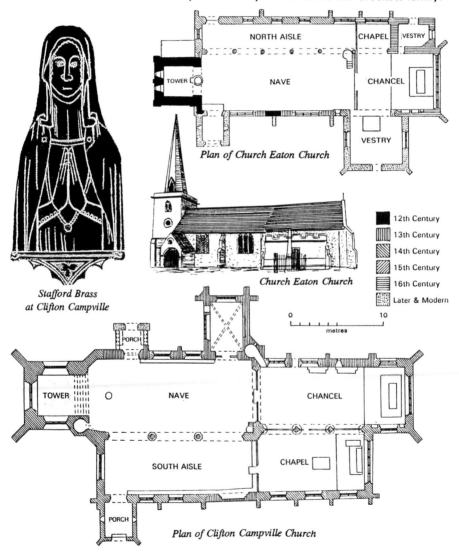

*Stafford Brass
at Clifton Campville*

Plan of Church Eaton Church

Church Eaton Church

- ■ 12th Century
- ▦ 13th Century
- ▨ 14th Century
- ▧ 15th Century
- ▤ 16th Century
- ▦ Later & Modern

0   10
metres

Plan of Clifton Campville Church

CLIFTON CAMPVILLE   *St Andrew*   SK 253108

There are indications that in the late 13th century the church was an aisle-less cruciform building. From it there remain parts of north walls of the nave and chancel with small buttresses, part of the south transept end wall, and the north transept which contained a dwelling with a latrine over a vaulted lower chamber now used as a vestry. A stair in the nave NE corner served both the upper chamber and the former rood loft. In the early 14th century the chancel was extended to the east by one bay with diagonal buttresses and a three bay chapel added on the south side with its south wall flush with that of the former transept. The transept itself was absorbed into a new south aisle with a three bay arcade. Of the same period or just slightly later are the south porch and the splendid west tower with a thin recessed spire supported by flying buttresses. The spire top fell down during a storm a few years ago. The chancel arch and its screen, and two windows in the chancel north wall are 15th century. Only the north porch is Victorian.

The chapel screens are of the 14th century and 1634 respectively. The chancel has early 14th century stalls with miserichords with foliage and heads. In a recess in the end wall of former south transept is a 14th century mural of Christ seated in glory with two kneeling donors. In the south chapel is a brass of c1360 depicting the upper half of Isabella Stafford on a bracket. The stem and surrounding canopy are missing. On the back has been discovered part of an earlier figure of a knight. Also in the chapel is a fine alabaster monument to Sir John Vernon, d1545, and his wife, with figures and shields along the sides. There are monuments to Sir Charles Pye, d1721, Sir Richard Pye, d1724, and Sir Robert Pye, d1736.

Clifton Campville Church

Church Eaton Church

CODSALL   *St Nicholas*   SJ 866040

The only features to survive the rebuilding of 1846-8 are the 15th century west tower, the reset Norman south doorway with chevron ornament and one order of columns with beaded trails on the capitals, and a recumbent effigy of Walter Wrottesley, d1630.

COLTON   *St Mary*   SK 047204

The west wall of the south aisle is early 13th century. Of the mid to late 13th century are the west tower with twin lancet bell-openings and the south chapel with its three bay arcade. The pinnacles on the tower are 15th century. All the rest was rebuilt by G.E.Street in 1850-2.

COLWICH   *St Michael*   SK 010210

Much of the church dates from a rebuilding in the 1850s but the nave and south aisle west walls, the four bay arcades, and the eastern parts of the large chancel are 13th century. The north aisle was rebuilt wider in the 15th century, and in 1640 the west bay was replaced by a high NW tower. There is a monument with a recumbent effigy of Sir Robert Wolseley, d1646. There are tablets to Gabriel Wood, d1706 and Charles Trubshaw, d1772.

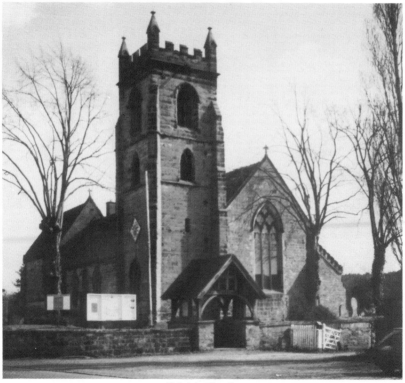

Colwich Church

COPPENHALL *St Lawrence* SJ 907194

This is an interesting specimen of a small, almost unaltered, chapel of c1200-25. It was a chapel-of-ease to Penkridge until the 19th century. The nave has three lancets in each side (those on the south are of 1866, replacing two 18th century windows) a west doorway, and a blocked south doorway, whilst the chancel has two south lancets, and three lancets with a round window above in the east wall. The timber framed belfry on the west wall is 16th century.

CRESWALL SJ 896040

In a field are ruins of the chancel north and east walls with two 13th century lancets and the outline of a larger later window.

CROXALL *St John the Baptist* SK 197137

There is no village, and the church has only the hall for company. Some of the chancel masonry including the priest's doorway is of c1200, and the nave west wall and tower are 13th century. The tower rather oddly rises from a wider rectangular lowest storey. The eastern part of the chancel is early 14th century. The north wall of the nave is 15th century, and the south wall has medieval windows reset in the 18th century in the three blocked arches of an arcade for an aisle then pulled down. The chancel is almost completely paved with a fine series of incised slabs dating from c1480 to the 17th century and commemorating the Curzon and Horton families. There are also many memorial tablets.

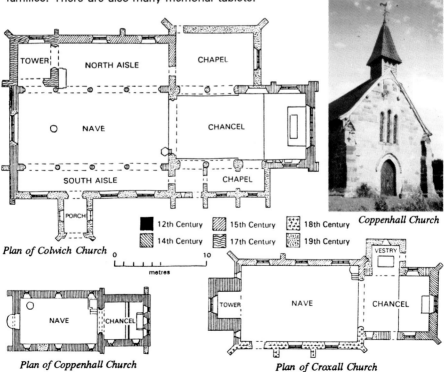

Coppenhall Church

Plan of Colwich Church

12th Century   15th Century   18th Century
14th Century   17th Century   19th Century

Plan of Coppenhall Church

Plan of Croxall Church

Dilhorne Church

DILHORNE   *All Saints*   SJ 971433

The four bay arcades are late 13th century, although the present aisles are of 1819. The chancel is 15th century and contains a Jacobean communion rail. Of much greater interest is the unusual 13th century octagonal west tower with a 15th century top stage with two-light windows and a plain, flat top.

DOSTHILL   SK 213998

To the north-east of the parish church of 1870-2 is the small and little altered nave of the original Norman church. It has original north and south doorways, a single narrow window in each of the north, south, and west walls, and the east wall has a four light 16th or 17th century window set in the blocked chancel arch.

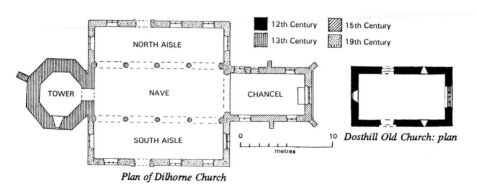

Plan of Dilhorne Church

Dosthill Old Church: plan

DRAYCOTT-IN-THE-MOORS   *St Margaret*   SJ 982403

The aisled nave and the chancel were rebuilt in the 19th century, so only the west tower of c1300 with a later bellstage and the Draycott chapel on the north side of the chancel are old. In the chapel are effigies of a cross-legged knight of c1300, Sir Philip Draycott, d1554, John Draycott, d1604, and their wives, and Richard Draycott, d1662. There are also tomb chests without effigies to Richard Draycott, d1544, and Philip Draycott, d1604, and several incised slabs.

DRAYTON BASSETT

St Peter   SK 193002

The nave of 1793 has a short chancel of c1855. At the west end is a 15th century tower. This served as a porch on the south side of the fine 14th century church of five bays with three-light side windows and a six-light east window. The SW corner of the old nave adjoins the tower NW corner.

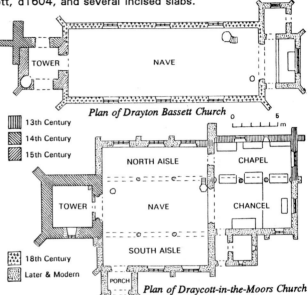

Plan of Drayton Bassett Church

13th Century
14th Century
15th Century
18th Century
Later & Modern

Plan of Draycott-in-the-Moors Church

Draycott-in-the-Moors Church

St Edmund's Church, Dudley   *Eccleshall Church*

DUDLEY   *St Edmund*   SO 946904

Of 1722-4, but somewhat altered in the mid 19th century, especially inside, are the brick and stone nave with round arched windows, the west tower, and the unusually long chancel. There are flat ceilings with coved edges. There are two Jacobean chairs in the chancel and parts of a three decker puplit also remain, together with fragments of an 18th century oak reredos. The church stands on the site of the eastern half of a large medieval building of which traces have been found below the crypt under the tower. It was destroyed in 1646 by Colonel Leveson, but ruins of it remained until 1724.

DUNSTON   *St Leonard*   SJ 928177

This building, a chapel-of-ease to Penkridge until the 19th century, is first mentioned in 1445 and was probably first erected about that time. It was rebuilt in the 18th century except a small west tower with the lower stage double stepped on the north and south sides. An account of 1843 indicates that there was no access to the tower except by means of its west doorway and that the church contained no monuments. The existing church is entirely of 1876-8, with a vestry added in 1907.

ECCLESHALL   *Holy Trinity*   SJ 828292

The Bishops of Lichfield owned Eccleshall and often resided at the nearby castle. This explains the generous size of the 13th century church of which there remain the west tower with original arches to the east, north, and south, five bay arcades, and the chancel with its clasping buttresses and lancet windows. On the north side of the chancel is an original treasury or vestry, lighted only by narrow lancets and only entered from the chancel. Of the 15th century are the wide south aisle and porch, the clerestory of three light windows, and the tower top with a lozenge frieze and eight pinnacles. In 1866 G.E.Street rebuilt the parts of the original narrow aisles which remained flanking the tower, the whole of the north wall, the chancel arch, and the chancel east lancets. The font is 13th century and there are fragments of a Saxon cross shaft in the vestry. There are two incised slabs on tomb chests by the tower to Bishop Sampson, d1554, and Bishop Bentham, d1578. In the chancel is a tomb chest with a recumbent effigy of Bishop Iverin, d1609 with kneeling figures of his wives nearby. See photograph on page 6.

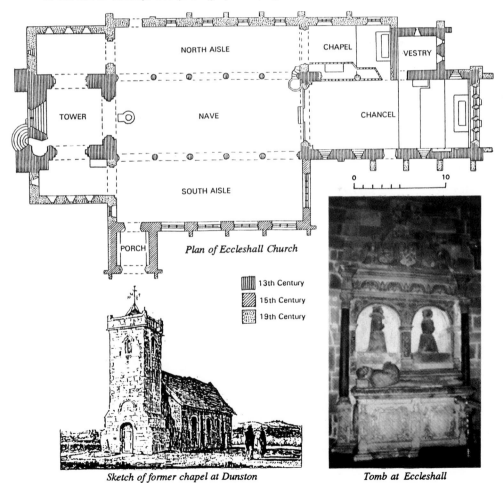

NORTH AISLE

CHAPEL

VESTRY

TOWER

NAVE

CHANCEL

SOUTH AISLE

PORCH

0   10

Plan of Eccleshall Church

13th Century
15th Century
19th Century

Sketch of former chapel at Dunston

Tomb at Eccleshall

ELFORD *St Peter* SK 185106

Except for the 14th century chancel east wall and the west tower dated 1598 (perhaps referring to repairs), the church was rebuilt by Salvin in 1848-9, and the south aisle and chapel were rebuilt by G.E.Street in 1869-70. The chapel was founded as a chantry in 1474. It contains a series of monuments which were restored in 1848. The figure of a knight of c1370 has an incorrect inscription calling him Sir John Stanley. There are also effigies of Sir Thomas Arderne, d1391, and his wife, the child John Stanley killed by a tennis ball c1460, and Sir William Smythe, d1525 and his wives. There is also a curious monument with the upper and lower parts only of an effigy in relief of William Staunton, c1450, and there are several incised slabs to various ladies of the period c1480 to 1540.

ELLASTONE *St Peter* SK 117435

The nave south wall, the wide north aisle, and the narrow western bays of the arcade are of 1830, but the two very wide eastern bays of the arcade are late medieval, and probably also of that period are parts of the chancel walls and the two bay arcade to the north chapel. The chancel and chapel east walls date from 1588, that year appearing on the chancel, and the tower has a large inscription with the date 1586. There are defaced effigies of Sir John Fleetwood, d1590 and his wife.

ELLENHALL *St Mary* SJ 841265

The brick west tower and nave were built by William Baker in 1757. The stone chancel has a Norman window but is mostly of the 15th century and 1683. The nave windows, the porch, and the vestry are all Victorian.

ENDON *St Luke* SJ 928538

The west tower is of 1730. The nave was rebuilt in 1876 when a new south aisle and porch and also a new chancel were added.

Enville Church

Ellenhall Church

Ellastone Church

ENVILLE *St Mary* SO 824868

The four bay south arcade with round piers and square scalloped capitals is Norman, and the much restored north arcade is 13th century. The chancel was built by Roger de Birmingham, rector from 1272 to 1307, whose tomb lies on the north side of it. The south aisle was rebuilt about the same time and there is some glass of this period. In the 1870s Scott refaced nearly all the exterior walls and built a west extension. He also rebuilt the tower added at an unknown date in the west end of the south aisle, giving it a fancy top crown. In the chancel are stalls with late 15th century miserichords with carvings of Sir Ywain at the castle gate, a couple in a pew, dogs in combat with a bear, and a seated angel under a canopy. There are recumbent alabaster effigies of Thomas Grey, d1559, and his wife.

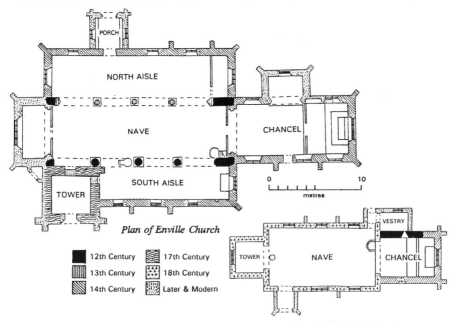

Plan of Enville Church

■ 12th Century	▨ 17th Century
▥ 13th Century	▦ 18th Century
▧ 14th Century	▨ Later & Modern

Plan of Ellenhall Church

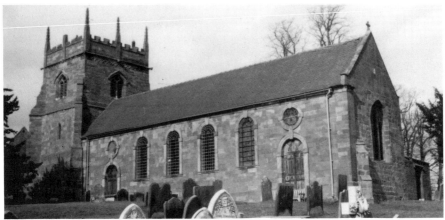

Forton Church

FAREWELL   *St Bartholomew*   SO 084117

In c1140 Roger de Clinton, Bishop of Lichfield, founded a priory at Farewell. A short section of masonry with one small window by the organ and pulpit may be a relic of the priory church of that period. The rest of the chancel is of c1300, although two side windows are later medieval, whilst the brick nave with a tower and porch set side-by-side at the west end is of 1745. An engraving of 1744 shows the church with holes in its roof. There are stalls with miserichords with foliage and the initials E.R. for Edward VI or Elizabeth I, and the communion rail has twisted balusters.

FORTON   *All Saints*   SJ 751213

The whole of the south side and the five bay north arcade with Tuscan columns on high plinths and round arches, plus the pulpit, font, and Royal Arms are of 1723. The work was presumably paid for by Acton Baldwin, whose arms appear in the middle of the south side. It makes an interesting contrast with the older work comprising the north and east walls of the chancel of c1200, the 14th century north aisle, and the tower, which is 13th century below and of c1500 above with a decorative frieze and pinnacles. The NE vestry is of 1842 but there was an older vestry on the site. The tomb of Thomas Skrymsher, d1633, with alabaster effigies and a flat canopy on four columns is by Garrat Hollemans. Part of a Norman font also remains, and there are hatchments to the Oakley and Boughey families, but stained glass with arms of Thomas de Bottetort in an aisle window has gone.

0 [_____] 10 metres

▦ 13th Century
▨ 14th Century
▧ 15th Century
▦ 18th Century
▦ 19th Century

TOWER   NORTH AISLE   VESTRY   NAVE   CHANCEL

Plan of Forton Church

FRADSWELL *St James The Less* SJ 992312

Until 1852, when the wide south aisle was added, and a vestry and two new north windows, this was a small church with a chancel of c1200 with two tiny lancet windows and two other windows of c1300, and a purple brick nave and west tower of 1764.

GAYTON *St Peter* SJ 978284

The 13th century chancel doorway is the only medieval feature which is visible externally as the brick west tower and nave north wall are of 1732 and the south aisle, chancel east end, and the vestry are of the 1870s. Inside, the chancel arch turns out to be Norman, although much restored, and there are four bay south and north arcades of the 13th and 15th centuries respectively. The north aisle was later removed and the arcade on this side has been blocked up. There are some medieval floor tiles and an old effigy of a man in civilian dress.

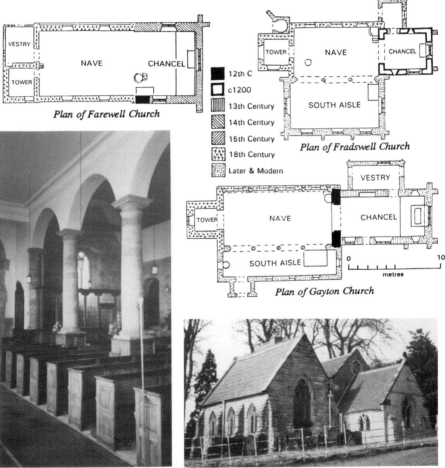

VESTRY NAVE CHANCEL TOWER

Plan of Farewell Church

■ 12th C
□ c1200
▥ 13th Century
▨ 14th Century
▧ 15th Century
▦ 18th Century
▨ Later & Modern

TOWER NAVE CHANCEL
SOUTH AISLE

Plan of Fradswell Church

VESTRY
TOWER NAVE CHANCEL
SOUTH AISLE

0   10
metres

Plan of Gayton Church

Fradswell Church

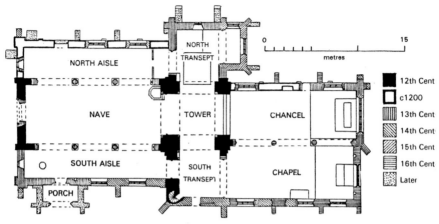

Plan of Gnosall Church

GNOSALL *St Laurence* SJ 830209

This interesting former collegiate church has a complex plan but is not particularly large. Of a cruciform Norman church there remain the four round arches of the crossing tower, the west wall of the nave, and part of the south transept. The latter has some remains of blank arcading at ground level and a triforium of two twin openings in the west wall. The western part of the chancel is also 12th century, or perhaps of c1200, which is the period of the north aisle outer wall. The three bay arcades, the south aisle outer wall, the north transept and the chancel east end are mid 13th century. The only part which is definitely 14th century is the main east window but the nave windows could be of that era, and perhaps the south transept end wall. During the 15th century the north transept was given a shallow east chapel. At about the same time or in the 16th century the tower was given a new top stage with a frieze of saltire crosses and eight pinnacles and the south chapel was extended to the same length as the chancel and given a new three bay arcade and a wide arch to the transept. It has been suggested that originally this building was a detached separate structure used to accommodate the four clergy. Victorian contributions are luckily confined to the south porch and most of the north side buttresses. During a restoration c1890 one arcade pier, which had been thinned to accommodate a gallery then being removed, collapsed, bringing with it two arches and part of the roof. Although heraldic glass to the Peshall, Harcourt, and Whitgreave families is recorded in the church in 1680, there are now no furnishings of historical importance. However there is an effigy of a child of c1380-1420 and an alabaster effigy of a knight of c1470, thought to be one of the Knightly family.

GRATWICH *St Mary* SK 029317

The brick nave with pointed windows and a bellcote was built in 1775. Although also of brick, the chancel is probably 17th century.

GRINDON *All Saints* SK 085545

This church of 1845-8 has a Norman font with a wavy ornamental band. Near it are two stone coffins. There are fragments of medieval glass in the porch.

Gnosall Church

Gnosall Church　　　　　　　　*West doorway, Gnosall*

Hamstall Ridware Church

HAMSTALL RIDWARE   *St Michael*   SK 106194

The west wall of the Norman nave survives with part of an upper window. In the 14th century a small west tower was added and the original modest chancel replaced by a larger one. A chapel was provided on the north side but its outer walls were rebuilt in the 18th century. In the 15th and 16th centuries the nave was given aisles with three bay arcades, that on the south extending further east along the south side of the chancel as a chapel and vestry. The chapel, however, may replace an earlier one. One of the two arches opening into it is four-centred and panelled and filled with a tomb chest of Richard and John Cotton, d1502. The side sections of the reredos with paintings of poor quality showing the life of Christ may be relics of a late 15th century screen or rood loft. Both chapels are divided from the aisles by 16th century screens. In the south chapel are fragments of 14th century glass.

Haughton Church

Interior of Hamstall Ridware Church

HANBURY   *St Werburgh*

SK 171279

Apart from some corework in the heightened west tower, and also the four bay 13th century arcades with round piers, the church was entirely rebuilt in the 1860s and 1880s. It has, however, quite a collection of interesting monuments. The cross-legged knight in the south aisle may be Sir John Hanbury, d1303. Of the same period is the slab with the heads of a husband and wife in rectangular recesses below a cross in relief. Below a removable section of the chancel floor is a small brass to a former rector, John Cheney, d1408. Also in the chancel are an incised slab to Ralph Adderley, d1595, and his wives, the reclining figure of Charles Egerton, d1624, the busts in architectural surrounds of Mrs Argade and her daughter, d1628 and 1657, and the recumbent effigy of John Egerton d1662.

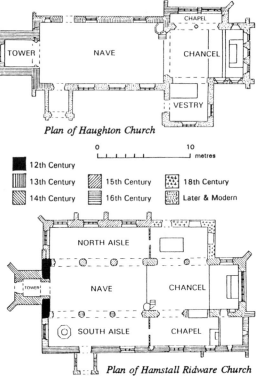

Plan of Haughton Church

0   10
|_|_|_|_|_|_|_|_|_|_| metres

■ 12th Century
▨ 13th Century
▨ 14th Century
▨ 15th Century
☰ 16th Century
▦ 18th Century
▩ Later & Modern

Plan of Hamstall Ridware Church

HANLEY   *St John the Evangelist*   SJ 883479

The present church in Town Road is of 1788-90 with a polygonal apse added in 1872. In the vestibule is a datestone of 1738 referring to an earlier chapel to the west built on the initiative of John Bourne, Town Clerk of Newcastle. It was enlarged in 1764 but by 1777 was damaged by mining subsidence.

HARLASTON   *St Matthew*   SK 215110

The timber belfry is contemporary with the church of 1882 built by Ewan Christian, but stands on the lowest stage of a 13th century tower.

HAUGHTON   *St Giles*   SJ 865205

Blocked lancets in the west wall show that the nave was originally 13th century. A tower added in the 14th century was rebuilt during the incumbency of Nicholas Graviner, rector from 1489 until 1520, to whom there is incised slab. The tower has a lozenge frieze and pinnacles at the top. At the same time the nave was refaced externally and given new windows on the north side and a narrow chapel of St Catherine built alongside the chancel. The chancel was shortened in 1740 and a brick south transept was added in 1838. The south side of the church was entirely rebuilt and the chancel restored almost to its former length in 1887 under the direction of J.L.Pearson. A fresco of St George and the Dragon has gone but there are fragments of heraldic glass in a north window to the Bourchiers and Harcourts.

High Offley Church

Himley Church

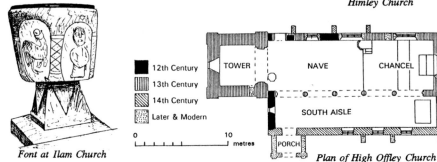

Font at Ilam Church

■ 12th Century
▦ 13th Century
▨ 14th Century
▦ Later & Modern

0 ┗┻┻┻┻┻┛ 10 metres

TOWER | NAVE | CHANCEL

SOUTH AISLE

PORCH

Plan of High Offley Church

HIGH OFFLEY   *St Mary*   SJ 748262

This is quite an interesting church, to which the Victorians have contributed only a south porch and two north windows. Part of the nave north wall is Late Norman with a doorway of c1200. The present chancel and south aisle, with a five bay arcade, were built in the early 13th century. Of a previous 12th century south aisle there remains the west wall with one window and the reused east respond of the arcade with two spiral volutes and a head. The lower parts of the west tower with clasping corner buttresses and the triple stepped lancets in the aisle east wall are late 13th century, and the reticulated east window of the chancel and the whole of the south wall of the aisle are 14th century. The chancel has a fine old roof with moulded beams. The tower top is 16th or 17th century. There are tablets to Jacobi Skrymsher, d1724, and Gerard and Catherine Skrymsher, d1700 and 1725 respectively.

HIMLEY   *St Michael*   SO 883912

The rendered west tower, the nave and apsidal chancel, and the gallery and pulpit are all of 1764, built under patronage of the Dudleys of nearby Himley Hall.

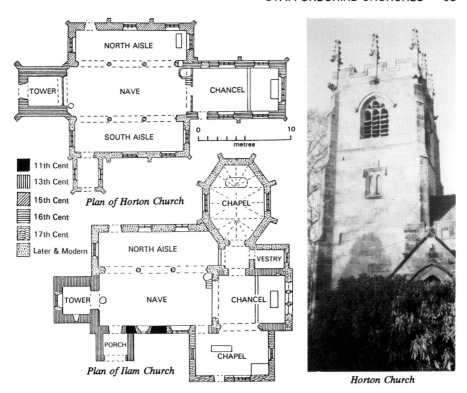

11th Cent
13th Cent
15th Cent
16th Cent
17th Cent
Later & Modern

Plan of Horton Church

Plan of Ilam Church

Horton Church

HORTON *St Michael* SJ 942574

The south aisle with its arcade and porch, and the east window of the chancel are of 1864. Otherwise the church is entirely late medieval. Probably the north aisle with a three bay arcade is late 15th century and the west tower and chancel are early 16th century. The screen closing off the tower base is of 1618, and there is a brass with kneeling figures of John Wedgwood, d1589, and his wife. There are two other monuments without effigies to men both also called John Wedgwood who died in 1724 and 1757 respectively.

ILAM *Holy Cross* SK 133507

Except for some 13th century walling in each side wall, the chancel is of 1855-6 when the north aisle was added. North of the chancel is the large octagonal chapel with many pinnacles erected in 1831 at the expense of Jesse Watts Russell to contain the effigy of his father-in-law David Pike Watts. The nave south wall has a blocked tall round-headed doorway which is likely to be Late Saxon, and a relic of a nave shorter than the present 13th century nave. The plain west tower and the south porch are also 13th century, and there is a south chapel bearing the date 1618 with ogee headed lights to the windows. The font is Norman and has beasts and barbaric figures. In the south chapel are the lowest part of a 13th century shrine of St Bertelin with a series of quatrefoil shaped openings, a Saxon stone fragment with interlace, alabaster effigies of Robert Meverell, d1626, and his wife, and a kneeling figure of their daughter. Two Late Saxon crosses lie in the churchyard.

Ilam Church

INGESTRE   *St Mary*   SJ 978247

The church lies close to the hall, far from any village. It is a great rarity in being a Wren London City type church bearing the date 1676 set out in the wilds of the country. Wren himself may have had a hand in designing it as he was an associate of Walter Chetwynd of Ingestre Hall. The church has a west tower with a top balustrade and four urns which contains in its base an oval entrance lobby reached through a doorway with Tuscan columns and a pediment. The nave has a flat stuccoed ceiling and aisles with arcades of four arches set on clusters of four shafts, and a clerestory of round windows. The chancel has a plaster tunnel vault and a very fine screen with the Royal Arms. The church is packed with monuments to the Chetwynds, Talbots, and Chetwynd-Tabots, but the only ones requiring a specific mention here are the diptych tablets in the chancel of 1663, 1667, 1692, and 1741. See the photograph on page 7.

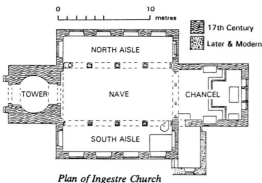

Plan of Ingestre Church

IPSTONES   *St Leonard*

SK 0185502

The present church was built for John Sneyd in the 1790s, and has a chancel of 1902-3. The 15th century windows and doorway are reset in younger walling. Inside is a Norman tympanum with dragons and an ornamental band.

KEELE *St John* SJ 810453

Within the church of 1868-70 designed by J. Lewis are the recumbent effigies of William Sneyd, d1613, and his wife, and an architectural tablet with two putti to Ralph Sneyd, d1703.

KING'S BROMLEY *All Saints* SK 122170

The Norman nave retains a small original south window. The chancel and wide north aisle with a three bay arcade and ogival headed north doorway, plus two south windows, are 14th century. The west tower and the clerestory of three light windows are 15th century. The south porch, the long organ chamber and vestry, and most of the features of the chancel are Victorian. The pulpit is dated 1656 but is heavily rebuilt, and the moulded font is of 1664. The chancel screen is unusual, having intertwined branches with leaves instead of tracery. There is some late 18th century glass in the vestry.

KINGSLEY *St Werburgh* SK 013469

The west tower is partly 13th century. The wide nave is of 1820, and the chancel and north vestries are of 1886.

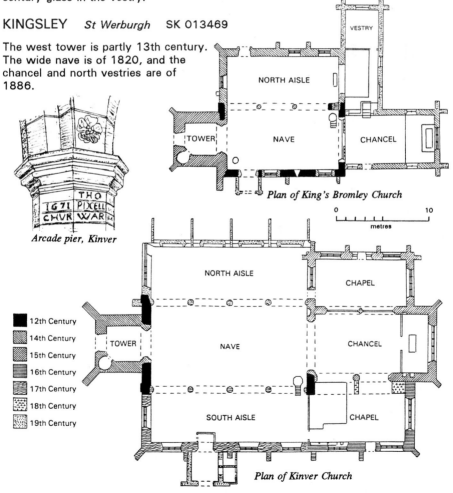

Arcade pier, Kinver

Plan of King's Bromley Church

12th Century
14th Century
15th Century
16th Century
17th Century
18th Century
19th Century

Plan of Kinver Church

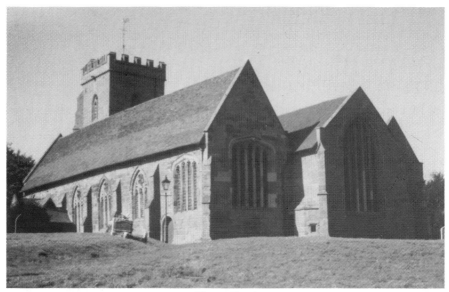

Kinver Church

KINGSWINFORD   *St Mary*   SO 894894

The overall impression externally is that of a Victorian church, but the west tower is at least partly Norman and there is a Norman tympanum of St Michael and the Dragon reset in the adjoining vestry in the SW corner. The chancel has some late 13th century masonry with one old window. The arcades, of four bays on the north and five bays on the south, appear to be facsimiles of originals of c1200 and the early 13th century. The font is dated 1662.

KINVER   *St Peter*   SO 846831

The church lies high up above the village on the side of Kinver Edge. Of a large Norman nave there remain three of the four corners, those on the west having pilaster buttresses. The west tower is an addition of the 14th century and the unusual font with a concave sided outline without breaks between the base, stem, and bowl is also of that period. The chancel and the Foley chapel on the north side, of three bays, but with only a two bay arcade, are 15th century. The fine nave roof is probably also of that period, although its design, without any east-west longitudinal beams, is an older type. The Grey chapel on the south side of the chancel is early 16th century. The placing of the ogival headed sedilia in the western bay suggests that that part was built first as an eastern extension to a lost medieval south aisle, and the eastern bay was an afterthought. The present south aisle, although it looks 14th century, is actually of 1671, the date that appears on the easternmost arcade pier. A north aisle was not added until 1856-7. Its arcade remains but the aisle itself was rebuilt in the 1970s, part of a Norman shafted window from the original north wall then being discovered. In the Foley chapel is the mutilated effigy of John Hampton, a courtier of Henry VI, d1472, and in the Grey chapel is a tomb chest with brasses of Edward Grey, d1528, in armour, and his two wives. The pulpit dates from 1625.

Kingswinford Church

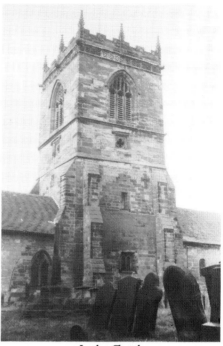

Lapley Church

LAPLEY   *All Saints*   SJ 873129

This church originally served a small priory founded at about the time of the Norman conquest as a dependency of an abbey in France. It was dissolved by Act of Parliament in 1414 during Henry V's wars against the French. The nave, central tower, and chancel remain in a much altered state of a 12th century cruciform church, only the transepts having been lost. The chancel has one original south window and in the 13th century was extended by one bay, doubling its length. The nave has some windows which may be 14th or 15th century and has on the south side signs of a blocked arch to a former chapel west of the lost south transept. The nave west end was refaced in the 19th century. The upper parts of the tower, with eight pinnacles and a decorative frieze are late 15th or early 16th century. In the 1630s the tower was provided with buttresses to give the support once provided by the transepts. There are two old screens, a Jacobean communion rail, a chancel door with four reset panels of c1535 with busts in medallions, and in the chancel floor is an incised slab.

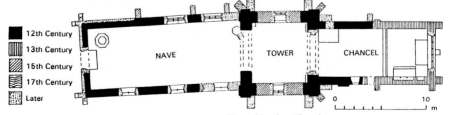

■	12th Century
▥	13th Century
▨	15th Century
▧	17th Century
▦	Later

NAVE   TOWER   CHANCEL

0   10   m

Plan of Lapley Church

LEEK   *St Edward the Confessor*   SJ 983566

The church has an interesting structural history. The Norman church was destroyed by a fire in 1297 and the oldest parts of the present building date from soon afterwards. They are the large west tower and the eastern parts of the aisles which then formed transepts with rose windows in their end walls. It may have been in the 15th century that the aisles were widened so that their outer walls were flush with the transept end walls. The nave roof with panels and bosses is early 16th century. The upper parts of the tower, with eight pinnacles, are probably of the same period. In 1556 the western two bays of the south aisle were taken down, and in 1593 the north aisle was similarly treated, leaving the central part of the church with wide aisles of three bays but with an unaisled western part connecting it to the tower. Older windows are reset in the 16th century walls of the unaisled part. The arcade piers are interfered with as a result of the insertion and removal of galleries. The south porch is of 1670 and the round arched churchyard entrance with a spiky top is dated 1634. The whole of the eastern part of the church was rebuilt in the 1860s by G E Street. In the church is a brass plate bearing kneeling figures of John Ashenhurst, d1597, and his wife. Outside in the churchyard are parts of two Late Saxon cross-shafts. One has a waist band and is over 3m long.

LEIGH   *All Saints*   SK 024358

The rebuilding by Thomas Johnstone in 1846 produced a cruciform church of a size far beyond the requirements of the village. Some old corework is said to survive in the upper parts of the tower and other old relics are the 14th century quarefoil shaped font, stained glass of the same period including a Crucifixion, and a tomb chest of alabaster for Sir John Ashenhurst, c1520, with pairs of canopied figurines.

Leek Church

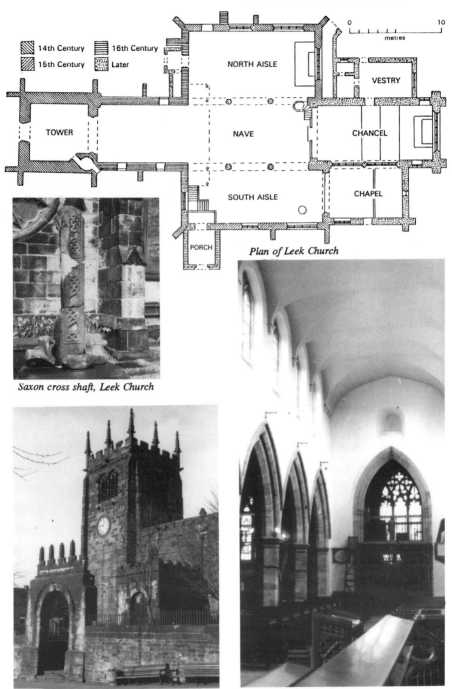

14th Century
15th Century
16th Century
Later

TOWER

NORTH AISLE

VESTRY

NAVE

CHANCEL

SOUTH AISLE

CHAPEL

PORCH

0   10
metres

Plan of Leek Church

Saxon cross shaft, Leek Church

Leek Church

Interior of St Chad's Church, Lichfield

St Chad's Church, Lichfield

LICHFIELD   *St Chad*   SK 122103

The church lies by a lake outside the town. The south aisle has Norman masonry and may represent the original building. The five bay south arcade with hexagonal pillars, and the fine doorway and the windows on the south side are 13th century. There are signs that this side then had a series of cross-gables instead of the usual longitudinal roof. The chancel is also 13th century and has an east window of c1300 with intersecting tracery. The west tower is 14th century and two chancel windows and perhaps the north arcade are 15th century. The brick clerestory and the nave ceiling are repairs made after the Civil War, when the church was occupied by Parliamentary troops and severely damaged. The north aisle was rebuilt in 1848, and the porch and vestry are also Victorian. The panelled font with shields is 15th century.

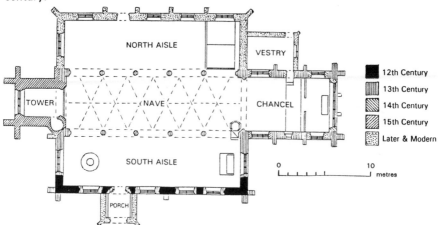

Plan of St Chad's Church, Lichfield

LICHFIELD *St Mary* SK 117096

This church lies by the market place in the middle of the city. The medieval church was entirely replaced by a classical style building probably designed by Lord Grimthorpe in 1717-21. In 1852 G.E.Street added a large west tower with a lofty spire, and in 1868-70 rest of the building was rebuilt on a generous scale in the style of c1300 to a design by James Fowler. No pre-Victorian monuments or furnishings survive. The church now serves as a day centre and gift shop.

LICHFIELD *St Michael* SK 124095

The church lies on a hill high above the city centre. Much of it dates from the rebuilding of 1842-3 by Thomas Johnson, and from a restoration in 1890-1, but the chancel has some 13th century masonry inside, and the west tower and perhaps the north arcade are 15th century. The font of 1669 has fleur-de-lis and Tudor roses. In the chancel is an effigy of a man in civilian dress, said to be a 14th century lawyer. There are arms of Queen Anne dated 1711.

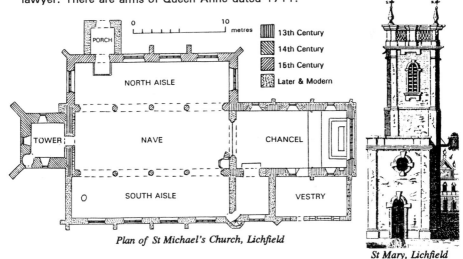

Plan of St Michael's Church, Lichfield

St Mary, Lichfield

St Chad's Church, Lichfield

LONGDON   *St James*   SK 082141

This church is quite an interesting one. It has a Norman nave with a south doorway and chancel arch both having two orders of columns and chevrons. On the chancel arch the chevrons are at right-angles to the main wall face, indicative of a date not earlier than c1175. In the early 13th century two of the original small round arched windows in the side walls at the west end were replaced by tall lancets, and later in the century a larger new chancel three bays long was built. In the 14th century the chancel was remodelled and given a new east window with reticulated tracery. The lowest stage of the tower, with diagonal buttresses, is also 14th century, but the top part is later. John Stoneywall, later Abbot of Pershore, built the embattled south chapel c1500. It has two heavily moulded four-centred arches towards the nave. A Norman font with a very stylized top band of interlocked palmettes and diagonal reeding is now supported on a 13th century capital from Lichfield Cathedral. In the chapel is a monument by Stanton to Thomas Orne, d1716.

LONGNOR   *St Bartholomew*   SK 089650

The single bodied church and west tower with an outer stair are of 1780, and the upper tier of windows were added in 1812 to serve galleries now mostly removed. The cauldron-shaped font is probably Norman, and has worn (probably recut) motifs.

LONGTON   *St John the Baptist*   SJ 910437

The present red brick nave and tower are of 1795 with transepts and a new chancel added in 1827-8. A chapel built here in 1762 was used by Anglicans although it was at first registered as being for Protestant dissenters. By 1792 it was described as decayed and too small for the growing congregation.

Madeley Church

MADELEY   *All Saints*   SJ 773444

Much of the church is later medieval, the west tower (embraced by the aisles), the
south aisle and the transepts being 15th century, and the north chapel (now the
vestry) and its screen being 16th century. However, the four bay north arcade with
pointed arches is Late Norman work of the 1190s, the north aisle with its NW
doorway and restored windows is 14th century, whilst the chancel was entirely
rebuilt in 1872 by Charles Lynam. The pulpit is Jacobean, the gallery in the tower
is of 1635, and there are an incised slab to Randolph Egerton, d1522 and his wife,
brasses depicting John Egerton, d1518 in civilian dress along with his wife, and an
architectural tablet to Sir Holland Egerton, d1730.

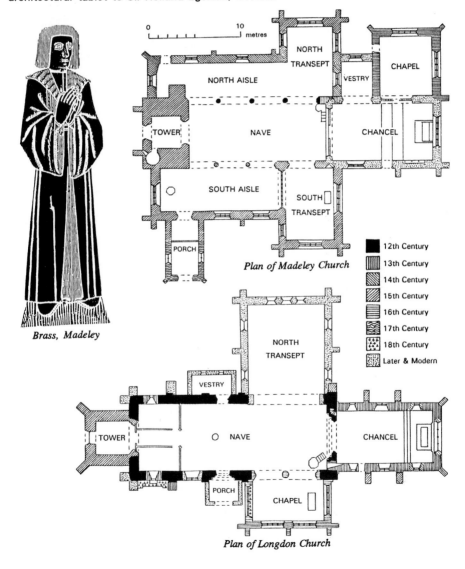

Brass, Madeley

Plan of Madeley Church

12th Century
13th Century
14th Century
15th Century
16th Century
17th Century
18th Century
Later & Modern

Plan of Longdon Church

Maer Church

NORTH AISLE

TOWER

NAVE

CHANCEL

SOUTH AISLE

PORCH

0   10
metres

■ 12th Century
▦ 13th Century
▨ 14th Century
▤ 16th Century
▒ Later & Modern

Plan of Mayfield Church

MAER   *St Peter*   SJ 793384

Most of the church, which has a west tower, nave, chancel, south porch and a north aisle continued eastward by vestries, appears to be early 17th century. The tower is said to have once borne the date 1610 upon it, but is still in the late medieval style. The south doorway with one order of colonettes is a relic of an original church of c1200-10, and the east and south walls of the chancel, and the windows in the aisle are Victorian. There are recumbent effigies of Sir John Bowyer, d1604 and his wife.

MARCHINGTON   *St Peter*   SK 138308

The church is a brick structure of 1742 designed by Richard Trubshaw, but with a chancel gothicised by the Victorians. An avenue leads to the west doorway of the tower, which has an octagonal top stage and cupola. The doorway has alternating rustication, which is also found on the four windows on the nave south side. There is an incised slab on a tomb chest to Walter Vernon, d1593 and his wife, and on the floor is an earlier incised slab of a man in civilian dress and his wife.

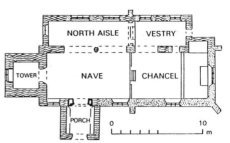

Plan of Maer Church

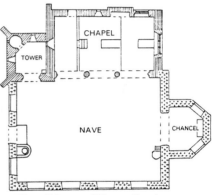

Mayfield Church

MARSTON   *St Leonard*   SJ 921277

The brick chancel and the nave windows are of 1794 to a design by William Dudley, but the nave masonry is either older or is re-used earlier material.

Plan of Mavesyn Ridware Church

MAVESYN RIDWARE   *St Nicholas*   SK 082168

The 13th century north aisle has a number of original lancet windows and a 15th century tower at its west end. A new wide nave and a small polygonal apsed chancel were built in 1782, replacing the original nave and south aisle and a late 13th century chancel with windows having trefoils over paired lancets. Shortly afterwards the many monuments were tidied up and displayed in the aisle along with bogus reliefs. One tomb chest bears the effigy of Sir Robert Mavesyn, killed at the battle of Shrewsbury in 1403, and another has an incised slab to Thomas Cawarden, d1593, and his wife. There are also effigies of two 13th century knights. On the floor are a series of incised slabs to David Cardon, d1557, John Cardon, d1477, John Cardon, d1485, and Hugh Davenport, d1473, with their wives. A helmet, sheaths and shield also lie in the aisle. A photograph of the church lies on page 7.

MAYFIELD   *St John the Baptist*   SK 154147

The south aisle dates from the late 12th century and has a doorway with columns and chevron and pellet ornamentation. The arcade is of three wide bays on round piers with scalloped capitals and square abaci. The aisle windows and the chancel are early 14th century, the porch is of c1600, and the south aisle battlements are Georgian. The north arcade is early 13th century but the aisle itself was rebuilt much wider than before in 1854. The font bears the date 1514, and the west tower is dated 1515. The fine benches are dated 1630 and 1633, and the pulpit and chancel panelling are of the same era, whilst the communion rail is slightly later.

MILWICH   *All Saints*   971320

The 15th century west tower appears to have stood at the NW corner of the medieval nave, the south wall of which collapsed in 1791. A new church of purple brick was built in 1792. Inside is a 12th or 13th century tub-shaped font with roll mouldings and traces of former blank arcading later chipped off.

MUCKLESTONE   *St Mary*   SJ 725374

The west tower is 14th century. The interior masonry of the nave, chancel, and north aisle may be medieval or of 1790, but the outside facing and all the other features belong to a rebuilding by the architects Lynam and Rickman in 1883.

NEWCASTLE-UNDER-LYME   *St Giles*   SJ 847461

A church here is first mentioned c1180. Until the early 19th century it was a chapel-of-ease to Stoke-on-Trent. By the 14th century it was a large building with a substantial west tower of c1300 and a north aisle. The oldest of four chantry chapels in the church was that founded in 1318 by the merchant William Swanild. Damage estimated at £3,115 was caused to the church in a riot in 1715, and in 1720-1 it was entirely rebuilt except for the west tower. It then had a broad nave of brick and stone able to seat 892 people and an east apse. In 1873-6 the church was again except for the tower entirely rebuilt and lengthened under the supervision of Sir George Gilbert Scott. The tower was repaired in 1841 and 1873, and in 1894 was refaced and given its present top. The font given in 1733 by Samuel Bagnell still remains, and there is a very defaced effigy of a civilian which was discovered in 1848. There are also seven 18th century memorial tablets. A carved fragment of 1733 showing a pelican in her piety by Peter Meredith from the old roof now forms part of the lectern. Newcastle also once had a chapel of St Mary west of the castle pool which presumably served the castle garrison. It is mentioned in 1297, but seems to have vanished by 1608 when it was referred to as a "late church".

Tower of St Giles' Church, Newcastle   *St Giles' Church, Newcastle-under-Lyme before it was rebuilt.*

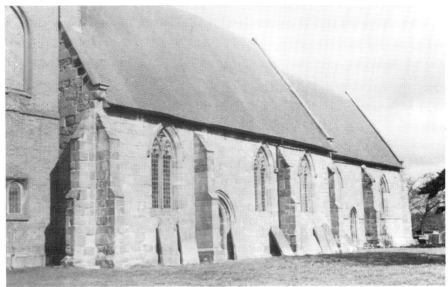

Norbury Church

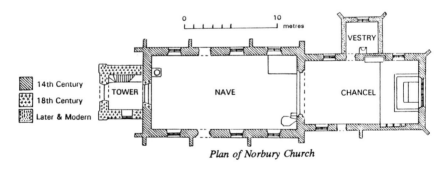

14th Century
18th Century
Later & Modern

Plan of Norbury Church

NORBURY *St Peter* SJ 788235

The wide but unaisled nave and chancel of closely fitting sandstone blocks are of c1340. They have trussed rafter wagon roofs and windows with a liberal use of hoodmoulds. A west tower and spire were built at the same time but the existing tower with pinnacles instead of a spire was built in 1759, probably to a design by William Baker. It was probably then that the north and south doorways were blocked up and the tower base became the entrance porch. The north vestry is of 1826-9 and the east window is also 19th century. The effigy of a cross-legged knight in the chancel under a splendid arch with ogees and pinnacles must be the person who paid for rebuilding the church, presumably Ralph Botiller the younger, d1342. The Botiller arms appear on a spandrel in the triple sedilia on the chancel south wall. Three other fragmentary effigies, probably of Sir Edward Botiller, d1412, and his wife and mother, were discovered in the 1820s. There is a fine brass of c1360 depicting the upper half of Lady Hawys Botiller on a bracket with part of a canopy above, and there is a tablet to Charles Skrymsher, d1708. There is also an old chest.

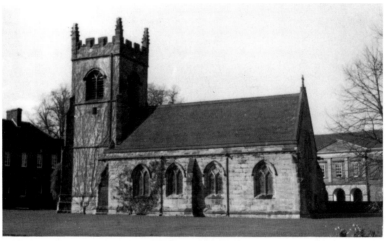

Okeover Church

NORTON-IN-THE-MOORS   *St Bartholomew*   SJ 894515

The church lies on a hill with a wide vista to the east. It is a brick building of four bays with square arcade piers and a west tower and was erected in 1737-8 to a design by Richard Trubshaw. In 1914 transepts and a new chancel were added to a design by J H Beckett.

OKEOVER   *All Saints*   SK 158482

Strictly speaking this was a private chapel belonging to the adjacent hall. The main body has diagonal corner buttresses and is undivided except by a screen. It appears to be entirely 14th century but parts of it must actually be later as an engraving of 1684 shows the church as having a south aisle which has now vanished. The diagonally buttressed west tower of c1500 is shown on the print with different details. It now has an embattled top with pinnacles. Fragments of an interesting brass are now set on a board after being recovered many years ago from a thief who was melting it down. The brass was originally engraved to depict William, Lord Zouche, d1447, in armour and his wives, but it was re-labelled and some parts turned over and re-engraved to commemorate Humphrey Okeover, d1538.

ONECOTE   *St Luke*   SK 048551

The west tower, the nave with arched windows, the short low chancel with a Venetian east window, and the pulpit and commandment board are all of 1753-5.

PATSHULL   *St Mary*   SJ 801008

The church lies in the grounds of the hall. Both were designed by Gibbs, but the church was built first and was consecrated in 1743. It consists of a west tower, a three bay nave with a pedimented projection in the middle of the south side, and a short chancel. The north aisle, the vestry, and the cupola on the tower were added in the 19th century. Two monuments predate the church, those of Sir John Astley, d1532, and Sir Richard Astley, d1687, and their wives.

PATTINGHAM *St Chad* SO 821992

The nave is very small and must have originally been Late Saxon or Early Norman, although the earliest surviving masonry is the two bay north arcade of c1180. Quite out of scale with the nave is the fine three bay 13th century chancel with lancet windows separated by buttresses with chamfered corners. The church is now quite wide on account of the spacious 14th century south aisle which embraces the tower of the same period and the first bay of the chancel, and also because of the outer north aisle with vestries at either end added in 1865. At that time the south arcade was renewed and the south porch added. The small fluted octagonal font is probably of the 1660s.

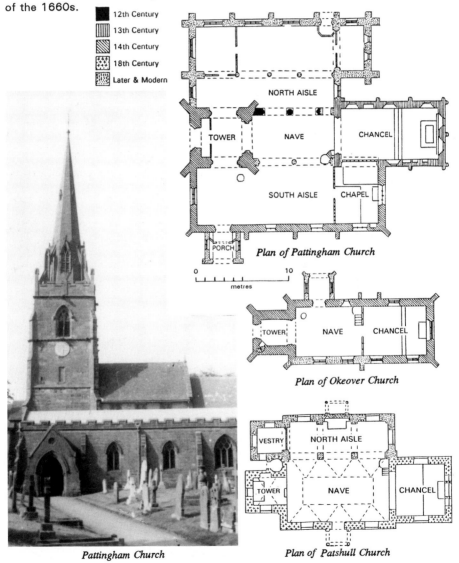

12th Century
13th Century
14th Century
18th Century
Later & Modern

NORTH AISLE

TOWER   NAVE   CHANCEL

SOUTH AISLE   CHAPEL

PORCH

Plan of Pattingham Church

0   10
metres

TOWER   NAVE   CHANCEL

Plan of Okeover Church

VESTRY   NORTH AISLE

TOWER   NAVE   CHANCEL

Plan of Patshull Church

Pattingham Church

PENKRIDGE   *St Michael*   SJ 922142

This church is remarkable in a number of ways. It served a large parish with numerous chapels of ease, some of which are now parish churches in their own right. It is a spacious building which formerly served a college as well as the large village. Being all embattled, the exterior looks mostly late medieval as one approaches the church from the east. In fact the four bay chancel arcades and much of the outer walling of the eastern parts is as early as the 1220s when Henry de London, retired Archbishop of Dublin, was Dean of the college, whilst the four bay arcades and most of the walling of the nave and aisles is of c1250. Fully aisled medieval chancels are rare in parish churches outside of large towns and that at Penkridge is an unusually early example. The nave and its aisles are wider than their counterparts to the east. This effect was further increased in the early 16th century when the east half of the south aisle was widened to create a chapel. Also 16th century are the buttresses on the north aisle, the clerestory, and the upper stage with eight pinnacles of the 14th century west tower and south porch. The chancel east window is also 14th century. The chancel north aisle still has typical 13th century pilaster buttresses but the south side was rebuilt in 1578, the priest's doorway having on it the name of the then vicar James Reddings. New windows of a debased gothic form were inserted at the same time. One of the south chapel buttresses is dated 1677, referring to repairs. Only the large NW vestry is new 19th century work, although the chancel arch was also raised during that period.

In the chancel are eight late 15th century stalls with miserichords decorated with foliage and a screens of the same period. The iron screen in the chancel arch is Dutch work of 1778 from Cape Town. The font by the south door is dated 1668 and has fleur de lis and the initials C.R. probably referring to Charles II. In the south aisle is an incised slab to Richard Littleton, d1518 and his wife Alice. There is an incised slab in the south chancel aisle to William Wynnebury, d1502, and his wife. In the chancel itself is another incised slab of the 1630s with kneeling children, plus monuments to four different Sir Edward Littletons of Pillaton Hall who died in 1558, 1578, 1610, and 1629 with their respective wives. The first two have recumbent effigies on tomb chests and the last two a combined two tier monument.

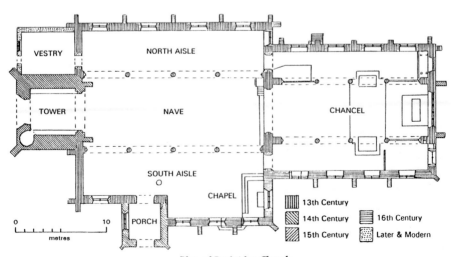

Plan of Penkridge Church

Penkridge Church

Penkridge Church

Penn Church

Cross, Rolleston

PENN   *St Bartholomew*   SO 894954

The church lies on the southern fringe of Wolverhampton with green countryside to the south. The three western bays of the five bay north arcade, and the west part of the much altered aisle, plus the decorated tiles on the chancel floor, are 13th century. The brick tower of 1765 is said to be actually a re-encased 15th century structure. The NW vestry is dated 1826, and the west part of the south aisle is of 1845. The nave and aisles were lengthened eastward and a new chancel and three bay south chapel were added in 1871-2. Immediately south of the church is the base and part of the round shaft of a Saxon preaching cross.

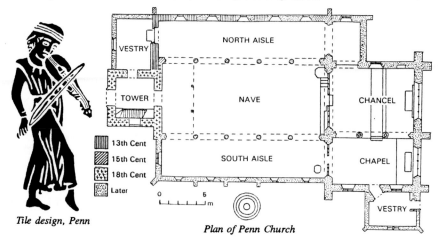

Tile design, Penn

Plan of Penn Church

PIPE RIDWARE   *St James*   SK 096178

A Norman font lies in the church of 1840, which has a chancel of 1899.

QUARNFORD   *St Paul*   SK 001664

This small remote church on the Cheshire border was rebuilt in 1754 and 1901.

RANTON   *All Saints*   SJ 855243

The 13th century nave has a group of three lancets at the west end. The side windows are 15th century, and the brick chancel is of 1753.

ROCESTER   *St Michael*   SK 113394

The 13th century churchyard cross with dogtooth on the shaft and a circular stepped base is a more important relic than the church itself, as the latter was entirely rebuilt in 1870 by Ewan Christian except for the 13th century west tower.

ROLLESTON   *St Mary*   SK 235277

The Norman nave retains original north and south doorways, the latter having an order of columns with scalloped capitals and a roll-moulding, whilst the former has been refaced. The chancel also has one Norman north window. Most of the windows, including some with reticulated and cusped intersected tracery, and one unusual example with a square head, are 14th century, the date of the west tower and south aisle. The aisle has only a two bay arcade but it extends west in front of the Norman doorway and eastward beside the chancel. The two bay north chapel with vestries east of it and the south porch are 19th century. The monument of Bishop Sherborne of Chichester, d1536, has a recumbent effigy let into a wall niche with the middle part of the body hidden by a block of stone with Renaissance motifs. The monument to Thomas Caldwell, d1554, and his wife was not made until c1600. There is an effigy of Sir Edward Moseley, d1638, and there are several incised slabs.

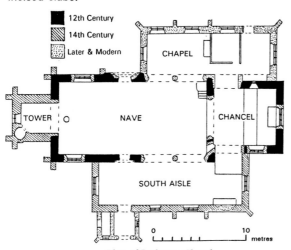

Plan of Rolleston Church

Rolleston Church

Rugeley Old Church

Old sketch of Rugeley Old Church

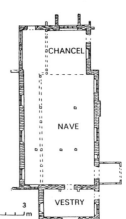

Plan of Rushton Spencer Church

RUGELEY　*St Augustine*　SK 045186

When a new church was built in 1822-3 on the other side of the road the 12th century chancel and the 13th century north chapel of the old church were walled off at the east end to form a mortuary chapel. A blocked Norman window is visible over the arcade between the chancel and chapel. The chapel has two 16th or 17th century windows on the north side. Inside is a brass to John Weston, d1566 and a tablet to Thomas Lauder, d1670. The rest of the church was left to decay and the nave south wall, the south porch, and the aisle north wall have now vanished. The 14th century tower with diagonal buttresses survives in a ruinous state and is connected to the chancel by an arcade of four bays. The middle bays are twice the width of those at the end, suggesting that as originally built in the 13th century the arcade was of six equal sized bays. A sketch made of the old church when it was still in use shows four dormer windows which presumably served a gallery, and blocked arches on the south side, relics of a former chapel or short aisle.

RUSHALL   *St Michael*   SP 024999

A 13th century font with dogtooth ornamentation lies in the church of 1856 designed by James Cranston. The spire on the SW tower was added in 1867-8.

RUSHTON SPENCER   *St Lawrence*   SJ 935621

This small church set alone on a hill beyond the north end of Rudyard Lake can only be reached on foot across a field. The stone exterior walls appear to be late 17th century, the east window being dated 1690 and the south doorway 1713. The church was then provided with a north aisle, a chapel on the north side of the chancel, and a western chamber which carries a timber framed belfry. The posts forming the arcades for the aisle and chapel appear to be relics of the original timber framed structure. The pulpit is late 17th century.

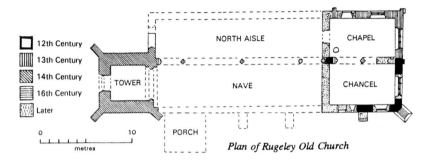

12th Century
13th Century
14th Century
16th Century
Later

0   10
metres

Plan of Rugeley Old Church

Rushton Spencer Church

SANDON   *All Saints*   SJ 954295

The church has a decidedly peculiar layout, especially at the west end. It is thought that the present south aisle, into which has been awkwardly inserted a small 15th century SW tower and adjacent 17th century entrance lobby. formed the whole church when it was built in the mid 13th century. Around 1300 a new narrower nave was built on the north side with a chancel the same width extending to the east. The nave is shorter at the west end than the aisle, but this may be because of 19th century rebuilding there. A short two bay aisle with windows with flowing tracery added on the north side of the new nave in the 14th century was remodelled inside in 1851 to serve as the family chapel of the Earls of Harrowby. East of it is a 19th century vestry. Parts of the chancel are 17th century and of 1782. Both nave and chancel have fine old arched braced roofs.

Although it looks Norman the font is in fact dated 1669. Fragments of the old screen are re-used in the chancel panelling. The reredos, pulpit, benches and altar table are 17th century. The west window has a fragment of 14th century glass and there is some 17th century heraldic glass in the east window. Four incised slabs made c1600 commemorate members of the Erdeswick family. There is a large monument with columns and a recumbent effigy of Samson Erdeswick, d1603, and a marble monument to George Digby, d1675.

SEIGHFORD   *St Chad*   SJ 882850

The church has a Norman chancel arch and a Norman north arcade of three bays with a wider fourth eastern bay indicating that there were once transepts. The aisle itself, the north chapel now forming an organ and vestry space, and the chancel windows are 15th century, whilst the chancel masonry is 13th century. The brick west tower now occupying what was the west bay of the nave, and also the nave south wall are 17th century work built after the fall of the Norman central tower. They were altered in 1748. The communion rail and pulpit are Jacobean, the font is of c1660, the squire's pew is of 1748, there are fragments of old glass in the chancel, and there are alabaster effigies of William Bowyer, d1593, and his wife.

Sandon Church

Shareshill Church

SHARESHILL   *St Luke*   SJ 944066

The lowest stage of the west tower is 14th century. From a tomb broken up in the 1740s are isolated alabaster effigies of Sir Humphrey Swynnerton, d1562, and his wife Cassandra. In their time the church finally attained full parochial status and the tower arch was blocked up except for a doorway and the existing tower top added. There is a tablet to Penelope Vernon, d1726. The church was given a new main body in 1742 with a semi-circular south porch with two pairs of columns, an apse with a Venetian east window, and a triple arched screen. Also of that period are the box pews, the pulpit, the communion rail, and the west gallery.

SHEEN   *St Luke*   SK 114615

The church itself was entirely rebuilt in 1850-2. In the churchyard just beyond the east end is a very worn effigy of a mid 15th century priest.

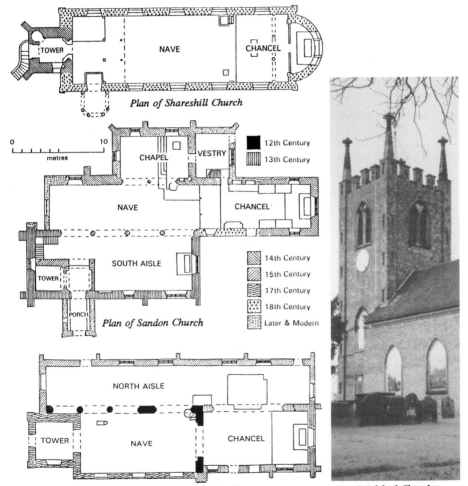

Plan of Shareshill Church

■	12th Century
▦	13th Century
▨	14th Century
▧	15th Century
▩	17th Century
▦	18th Century
▨	Later & Modern

Plan of Sandon Church

Plan of Seighford Church

Seighford Church

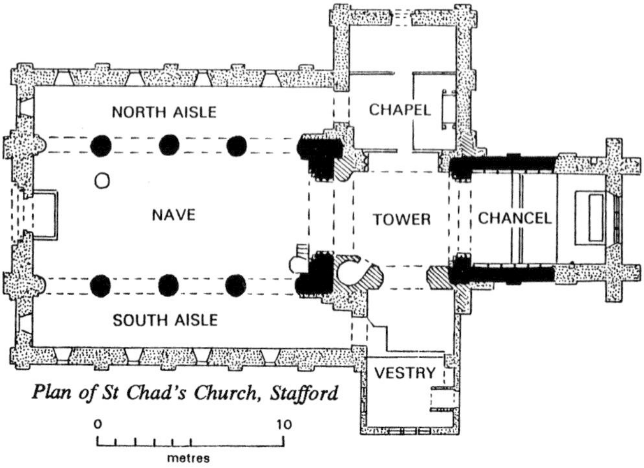

Plan of St Chad's Church, Stafford

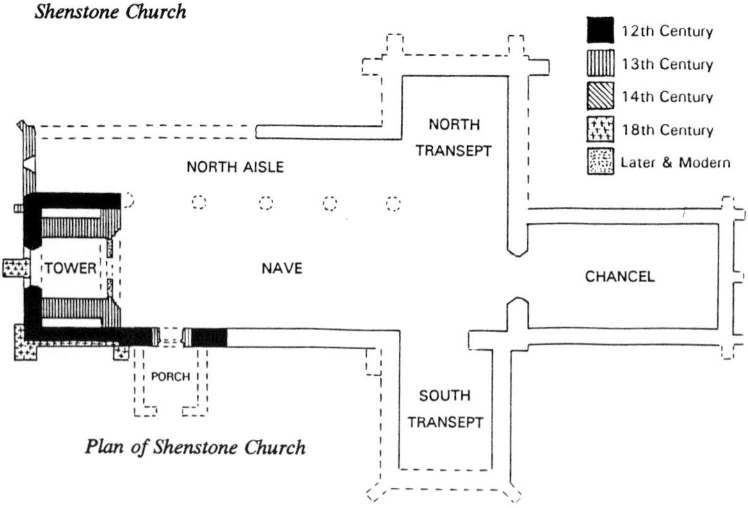

Shenstone Church

12th Century
13th Century
14th Century
18th Century
Later & Modern

Plan of Shenstone Church

SHENSTONE *St John* SK 110044

Near the hill-top church of 1852-3, in which is a 14th century font, are remains of the old church. Only the west tower, which is 13th century below, and 14th century above, with modern buttresses, and a short adjoining section of the nave with a 13th century doorway, stand high. There are also foundations of most of the rest of the church, but all signs of the 18th century south porch have gone. The south transept of c1300 served as the chapel of St Peter. The north aisle with a four bay arcade and a fifth bay which engaged the tower, and the north transept were 14th century. The chancel also appears to have been 14th century, although it retained the original narrow Norman chancel arch and was rebuilt in the 18th century when it was given a Venetian east window and a semi-circular gable above.

STAFFORD   *St Chad*   SJ 923232

Of the Norman church with an aisled nave of four bays there remain the arcades with clerestory windows above, plus the east and west arches of the central tower and the western part of the chancel with blind arcading inside. It does not appear that there were originally transepts. The arcade piers are sturdy and have multi-scalloped capitals and arches of two orders with chevrons. Chevrons and beak-heads proliferate on the western tower arch. A smaller new tower with its west arch immediately east of the Norman west arch was begun in 1394. Then or somewhat earlier the original apsed chancel was squared off by adding a new east end. The aisles were "swept away" in 1622 and for long the church lay ruinous. The west end was rebuilt shortly after it fell down in 1740 but it was rebuilt again in the 19th century. A new south aisle was built in 1874-5, a new north aisle in 1880, and a north transept was added in 1886. About the same time the ruined chancel and tower were put back into use. South of the tower is an organ and vestry space built in 1952-5.

St Chad's Church, Stafford

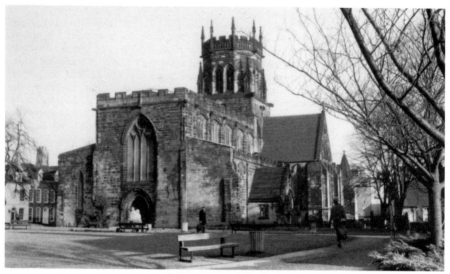

St Mary's Church Stafford

STAFFORD   *St Mary*   SJ 922232

Outside the west wall can be seen foundations of the Saxon church of St Bertelin, comprising a nave and narrower chancel. It was rebuilt in the 13th century as an adjunct of St Mary, and in the 14th century was given a south aisle and clerestory, and was only finally demolished as late as 1801.

St Mary's is essentially a 13th century building. The aisled nave, the lower parts of the crossing tower, and the south transept are all of c1210-30. The five bay arcades have square piers with four demi-shafts with renewed capitals, the originals having been hacked away for the insertion of galleries, now removed. In 1244 the Dean (St Mary's was collegiate) was given eight oaks from Cannock Forest towards the building of the belfry. A new chancel and south chapel divided by a five bay arcade were built in the 13th century, and a similar north chapel and a new north transept, larger than its southern counterpart and with boldly projecting diagonal buttresses and internal arcading, were built in the 14th century. The clerestory and north aisle windows are 15th century. In 1446 Henry VI licensed the Duke of Buckingham to found a chantry in the church but the only chantry known to have existed is that founded a few years later by Thomas Countin, Rector of Ingestre. However, as many as ten altars are recorded in the church in 1526. The north transept was then a Lady Chapel, but by 1548 had an altar to St Thomas Beckett.

Much damage was caused to the church in 1594 when the original spire fell down. The existing octagonal upper stage of the tower with eight pinnacles was built in the 1770s to a design by Richard Baker and Thomas Trubshaw. The church was restored by George Gilbert Scott in 1841-4, when the south transept and south chapel, plus the crossing arches were refaced and the south porch added in place of an 18th century Classical style one. Most of the old furnishings were then removed, a mayor's pew dated 1618 being removed to Grendon in Warwickshire. Prior to these works the seating faced westwards, not eastward as now. The quatrefoil shaped font with lions on it is of c1200. In the north transept are recumbent effigies of Sir Edward Aston, d1568, and his wife.

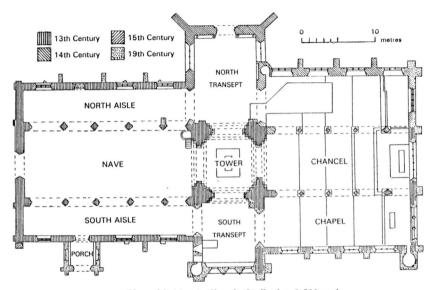

Plan of St Mary's Church, Stafford at 1:500 scale

Interior of St Mary's, Church, Stafford

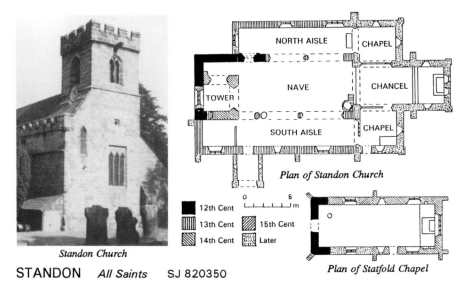

Standon Church

Plan of Standon Church

12th Cent
13th Cent   15th Cent
14th Cent   Later

0   5
m

Plan of Statfold Chapel

STANDON   *All Saints*   SJ 820350

The west wall and half of the north wall, including a shafted doorway, remain of the Norman nave. A north aisle with a two bay arcade was added in the 13th century. Later in the same century a south aisle with an arcade of three wide and high arches was built. In the 14th century a small tower was built within the west end of the nave, blocking half of the south arcade west arch, and having its own arches to the west and to a narrow passage left on the north side. The clerestory windows are 15th century but the other windows of the church, plus the chancel, side chapels, and the south porch are of the restoration by George Gilbert Scott in 1846-7. On the floor by the pulpit are fragments of a small rare cross brass of c1400.

STATFOLD   SK 238072

The plain doorway shows that the west wall of the chapel is late 12th century. The eastern half of the building is 14th century work and has two tomb recesses containing effigies of ladies of the 1390s holding hearts in their hands. The east window is 16th or 17th century, and the nave windows are of 1906. The font is Norman with a 14th century pedestal and a 17th century inscription. The pulpit is 18th century and there is some European glass of the 17th and 18th centuries in the east window, and an English medieval figure of a bishop in a south window.

STOKE-ON-TRENT   *St Peter ad Vincula*   SJ 879452

In a garden to the south of the new church built in 1826-9 are re-erected fragments of the old church demolished in 1830, with responds indicating the length of the north aisle. The fragments were recovered in 1881 from a watercourse serving Boothen Mill. The old church had a fully aisled 13th century nave probably of five bays, and a three bay chancel. Of the 14th century were the pinnacled west tower with pairs of angle buttresses and intersecting tracery in the west window, and the south porch and north vestry. A west gallery was inserted in 1717 and it seems that at the same time the nave and aisle roofs were lowered and a clerestory of small round windows was added, as shown in an sketch made c1824. On the pulpit of the new church is a small 17th century ivory crucifix, probably from Spain.

STONE *St Michael*   SJ 905338

The present tower was built in 1753-8 to a Gothic Revival style design by William Robinson, with William Baker supervising. The west tower is flanked by flat-topped parts with battlements, and the nave, also embattled, has two tiers of windows with Y-tracery. Original are the box pews, baluster font, and the galleries, except for their parapets which are Victorian. The chancel was remodelled in 1887. Below the tower are defaced 13th century effigies of a lady and a man in civilian dress. In the churchyard are two effigies to members of the Crompton family who died in 1606, and a mausoleum by Robinson and Baker to a member of the Jervis family.

STOWE-BY-CHARTLEY   *St John*

SK 003273

Both nave and chancel are Norman, the former having two original doorways with scalloped capitals and chevrons, and the latter having an original window and pilaster buttress on the south side. The north aisle and vestry were added in 1875 and the chancel arch was renewed about the same time. The west tower with a low but wide arch to the nave and a doorway with sunk-quadrant mouldings is 14th century, and also of that period are the nave south windows and the eastern part of the chancel. In the chancel are effigies of Sir Walter Devereux of Chartley Hall, d1537, and his two wives. The tomb chest has Early Renaissance ornamentation.

Stone Church

Doorway, Stowe-by-Chartley

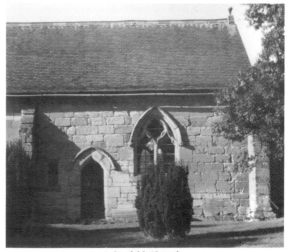

Statfold Chapel

Stretton Church

STRETTON   *St John*   SJ 887117

The Norman chancel has an original doorway and three small windows, plus a 14th century east window containing fragments of old glass. Stretton was a chapel-of-ease to Penkridge until the 19th century and it is possible that the chancel represents the whole of the Norman chapel. One pointer to this being the case is that what is now the priest's doorway had a timber porch in 1838, porches on chancels being very rare. A south vestry added in 1840 has now gone. The existing wide nave and shallow transepts are of 1860, but they replace a nave of 1753 with clasping west buttresses and two round headed south windows. There are 17th century chairs in the chancel, and there is an old chest.

Statfold Chapel

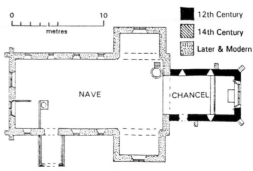

Plan of Stretton Church

SWYNNERTON   *St Mary*   SJ 853356

The architectural history of the church is not uninteresting but the chief feature to
see is the 2m high seated figure of Christ, a statue of high quality made c1260-80
brought in from a cathedral or abbey church. The Norman nave west wall survives,
with a doorway ornamented with beak-heads and a hoodmould with pellets. Later
in the 12th century a west tower was added. This in turn has a west doorway
(possibly reset from the nave) with one order of columns and chevrons on the arch.
Aisles with five bay arcades were added in the 13th century. The two eastern bays
of the south aisle were rebuilt as an embattled chapel in the 15th century and there
is a screen of that period with delicate tracery. The chapel and south aisle windows
were renewed in the 19th century when a south porch was added and the north
aisle entirely rebuilt except for the west wall. The chancel is late 13th century but
the north and east windows have been restored. The large chapel on the south side
of the chancel with defaced sedilia and a piscina is early 14th century. The effigy
of a cross-legged knight is thought to be Sir John de Swynnerton, c1254.

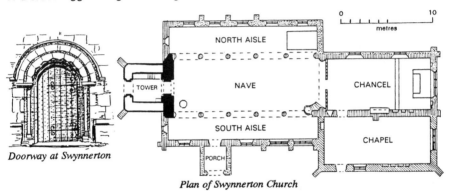

Doorway at Swynnerton

Plan of Swynnerton Church

Swynnerton Church

TAMWORTH *St Editha* SK 208041

This is the largest medieval parish church in Staffordshire, being marginally bigger than St Mary's at Stafford. A church has stood here since the 8th century. The remains of a former crossing tower and the western two thirds of the chancel with pilaster buttresses and one shafted window on the south side, both Late Norman, may lie on Saxon foundations. The Norman crossing still has original arches to former transepts on the north and south, but the arches to the east and west have been swept away. At the end of the 13th century a wide north aisle with a rib-vaulted porch was added. The church was damaged by fire in 1345, and between then and his death in 1369 Baldwin de Witney, Dean of the college attached to the church, erected an equally wide new south aisle, new finely moulded arcades off four bays with quatrefoil shaped piers, and the east bay of the chancel which has on the north side a doorway and three arches towards a spacious new chapel of St George on the north side. He also rebuilt the transepts, probably on the Norman (or even Saxon) foundations, since they were narrower than the nave and chancel, and projected less than the aisles. The south transept was absorbed into the 19th century extensions on the south side providing space for the organ and two vestries. A continuous series of 19th century restorations by Ferrey, Scott, and Butterfield saw the renewal of much of the outside of the church. Below part of the south aisle is a crypt of four bays which probably predates the fire, suggesting that there was a most modest aisle here beforehand. The clerestory and large west tower with heavy pinnacles are 15th century. The tower has the rare feature of a double spiral stair with two flights of steps starting at opposite corners and never meeting.

Except for part of an old font the furnishings are Victorian, but there are many old monuments. The effigy of a priest in the north chapel is likely to be Baldwin de Witney. There are also effigies of a lady of about the same period (c1370) and of a couple thought to be Sir Baldwin Freville, d1400, and his wife. Near them are alabaster effigies of Sir John Ferrers, d1512, and his wife. The defaced 15th century knight in the north transept may also be one of the Ferrers family, who then held Tamworth Castle. There are also Baroque kneeling figures of John Ferrers and his son Humphrey, d1680 and 1678, and a weeping putto with portrait medallion of John Horner, d1769.

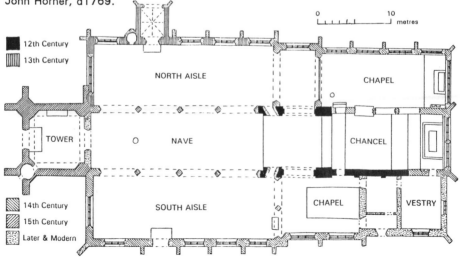

Plan of St Editha's Church, Tamworth at 1:500 scale

Tattenhill Church

Tamworth Church

TAMWORTH   *St James*   SK 209050

By Wigginton Rd is a small Norman chapel comprising just a nave and chancel which once served a hospital. It was given a new south doorway in the 13th century and a new west wall in the early part of the 20th century.

TATENHILL   *St Michael*   SK 205220

The doorways, especially the shafted one on the south side of the nave, indicate that the walls of the nave and chancel are 13th century. The chancel was given new windows in the 15th century (the east window is Victorian), and the nave was given new windows and buttresses in the early 16th century, to which period probably also belong the tower. Thus at a cursory glance the church looks younger than it actually is. It has a 13th century font and a rustic 17th century monument to the wife and family of Henry Griffiths.

TETTENHALL   *St Michael*   SJ 891003

Only the 15th century west tower and south porch of 1882-3 predate the rebuilding after a fire in 1950. Until then the church, which was collegiate, had a 13th century north arcade with 12th century responds, a 15th century clerestory, a font of the 1660s, and 13th century triple east lancets in each of Pendeford and Wrottesley family chapels flanking the south and north sides of the chancel. The latter contained the early 15th century tomb of Richard and Dorothy Wrottesley.

THORPE CONSTANTINE   *St Constantine*   SK 259087

The small estate church appears to be all of the rebuilding of 1883 but on closer inspection the west tower and spire turn out to be at least partly medieval.

TRENTHAM   *St Mary and All Saints*   SJ 865409

In 1833-42 Sir Charles Barry built a huge mansion (now demolished) for the 2nd of the Leveson-Gower Dukes of Sutherland on the site of an Augustinian priory founded c1150. From the priory church which survived at least in part until then came the round piers in the new church built by Barry close to the mansion in 1844, the Georgian west gallery, the Jacobean screens, the fragmentary effigy of a knight of c1215, and the large alabaster tablet with brasses of Sir Richard Leveson Gower, d1559 and his wife, who died in 1591. There are many 19th century monuments.

TRYSULL   *All Saints*   SO 852943

The western part of the north aisle and north arcade are late 13th century. Reset in the aisle wall is part of a Norman doorway. The chancel is early 14th century and so is the south arcade of three narrow and low arches, with a wider fourth arch to a former chapel. The aisle itself, and the eastern part of the north aisle, were rebuilt in the mid 19th century, whilst the south porch and vestry are later Victorian. The west tower, font, and nave roof with raking queen-posts and trefoils above the trusses, are 15th century. The screen is early 16th century, the pulpit is early 17th century, and there is amongst the Victorian glass in the east window some 14th century figures.

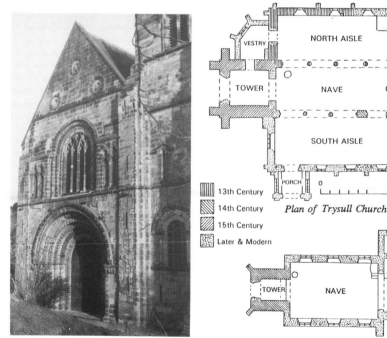

▥ 13th Century	
▨ 14th Century	
▧ 15th Century	
▦ Later & Modern	

Plan of Trysull Church

West front of Tutbury Priory Church   *Plan of Thorpe Constantine Church*

TUTBURY   *St Mary*   SK 211291

The church served a priory founded by Henry de Ferrers in the 1080s and lies below his castle high above the town. Nothing remains of the monastic buildings or of the crossing tower, transepts and eastern part of the church, now replaced by G.E.Street's chancel and apse of 1866. The nave and aisles are impressive early to mid 12th century work with truncated shafts of former vaults. The massive piers of the arcades of two orders with roll mouldings are circular at the east end but elongated quatrefoils towards the west. This end is later, and has a sumptuous west doorway of the 1160s with seven orders with beak-heads, and beasts and figures on the capitals. It includes some alabaster carvings, the earliest example of the use of this material in England. The south doorway is also a fine piece with two orders of columns and a lintel showing a boar hunt. Of the late 14th century are several windows and the tower built over the western bay of the south aisle. The north aisle outer wall is mostly the work of Joseph Bennett in 1820-22.

UTTOXETER   *St Mary*   SK 094335

The church is of 1828 by Trubshaw and Johnson with a chancel remodelled in 1877. Older are the early 14th century west tower with a recessed spire, the recumbent early 16th century alabaster effigy of a lady, remains of the alabaster tomb with an incised lid depicting Thomas Kynnersley, d1500, and his wife, the architectural monument to Edward Smith, d1753, and the 18th century plate. See the photograph on page 7.

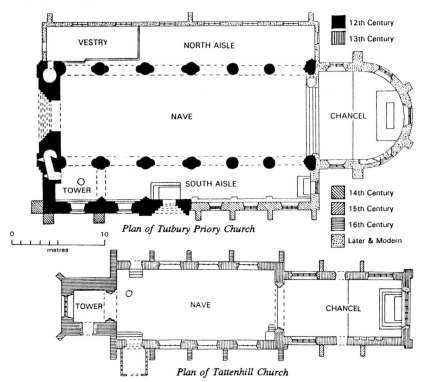

Plan of Tutbury Priory Church

Plan of Tattenhill Church

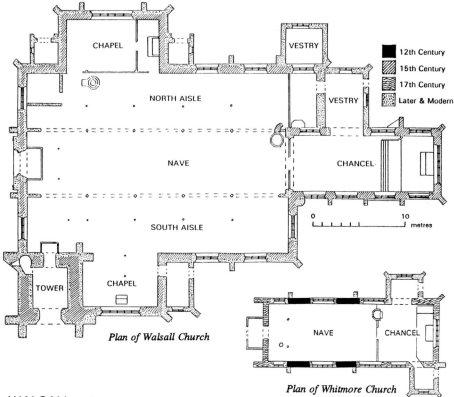

12th Century
15th Century
17th Century
Later & Modern

CHAPEL

VESTRY

NORTH AISLE

VESTRY

NAVE

CHANCEL

SOUTH AISLE

0   10
metres

TOWER   CHAPEL

Plan of Walsall Church

NAVE   CHANCEL

Plan of Whitmore Church

WALSALL   *St Matthew*   SP 051988

After rebuilding in the 1460s and 70s this hilltop church, once dedicated to All Saints, was a large building comprising a nave with wide aisles, outer chapels of St Clement and St Catherine on the north and south sides respectively, a SW porch-tower, and a long unaisled chancel. Little remains of it beyond the plan as the nave and its appendages were encased with fresh ashlar by Francis Goodwin in 1820-1, the chancel was heavily restored in 1877-80 by Ewan Christian, a choir vestry was added in 1908, and the tower and its recessed spire were mostly rebuilt in 1951. In the 1770s a Tuscan portico replaced the former porch in the middle of the west front. The arcade piers and window tracery in the nave and aisles are of iron. Below the chancel is a passageway and a crypt in two parts. The larger eastern section with an ashlar tunnel vault is mostly 15th century but possibly on 14th century foundations. The western part has two 13th century east lancets, showing that at that time the church was substantially shorter. Inside are a damaged effigy of Sir Roger Hillary, d1399, a 15th century font, and a set of eighteen 15th century stalls with miserichords carved with motifs such as a miller carrying a sack, a pelican, a musician, a man with a club, a centaur, several other beasts and several masks.

WARSLOW   *St Lawrence*   SK 087587

Nothing remains of the church of 1565. The existing four bay nave is of 1784, the tower is of 1820, and the chancel is of 1908. There is a damaged Norman font.

WATERFALL   *St James and St Bartholomew*   SK 082517

The west tower and nave with arched windows are of 1792. The 13th century chancel was mostly rebuilt in the 1890s, when the porch was added. The chancel arch and the inner arch of the south doorway are Norman. The communion rail, the font and the screen are 17th century.

WEDNESBURY   *St Bartholomew*   SO 987954

The church lies on a hill above the town. It looks much as it did c1800, although the aisled nave and north transept were renewed in 1827, the south transept and chancel were rebuilt by Basil Champneys in 1890, and the 14th century west tower has been refaced externally. There is a tablet with figures of Thomas Parkes, d1602, and his wife facing each other, and there are alabaster effigies of Richard Parkes, d1618, and his wife. The lectern is a late medieval carving of a cock, and the pulpit with blank arches and arabesque panels is of 1611.

WEDNESFIELD   *St Thomas*   SJ 945002

The church is of brick with a pedimented doorway and two tiers of aisle windows with Gibbs surrounds, and a west tower with a top balustrade. Parts of it are of 1751, but much of it was renewed by F.T. Beck in 1903 after a fire the previous year. He totally replaced the chancel built in 1842-3 by Wyatt & Brandon.

WEEFORD   *St Mary*   SK 142039

The church is of 1802 with a later chancel and bell turret extension. It has late 16th century glass in the Dutch Mannerist style brought here in 1803 from the chapel of the Duke of Orleans near Paris.

WEST BROMWICH   *All Saints*

SP 011930

Prior to a remodelling in the Classical style in the late 18th century and a total rebuilding by Somers Clarke in 1872, the church was dedicated to St Clement and had a west tower, north aisle, and chancel of the 14th century. North of the chancel was the Stanley chapel of c1530-50, whilst on the south side lay a chapel built in 1619 under the terms of the will of Sir William Whorwood. The only old relics now are parts of the inner walling of the tower including some Norman carved fragments, an octagonal font with shields in quatrefoils, a medieval chest carved out of a tree trunk, and two alabaster effigies thought to be Anne Whorwood, d1599, and Field Whorwood, d1658, now placed together on one tomb chest.

Walsall Church

WESTON-ON-TRENT   *St Andrew*   SJ 975271

The outer walls of the north and south aisles of the nave, and the very narrow three bay chancel aisles are Victorian, although late medieval windows are reset in the latter. The west tower is a fine 13th century piece with clasping buttresses and blank shafted lancets flanking the richly shafted bell stage lancets. The skeleton of the rest is of the same period, comprising three bay arcades in the nave, the chancel arch, and the chancel east end with three lancets separated by buttresses with their angles cambered off. In the tower are two bells of c1400. See photo on page 7.

WESTON-UNDER-LIZARD   *St Andrew*   SJ 806106

The church is physically joined on the south side to the house of Weston Park. It has a 14th century east wall and a 15th or 16th century west tower, but was otherwise totally rebuilt in 1700-1, when it was given a two bay south chapel to contain the Wilbraham family pew. The three bay vestry on the north, plus the coved wooden ceiling, are of 1876 by Ewan Christian. The fine pulpit and communion rail are early 18th century, and there are fragments of 14th and 17th century glass. In the chancel are two cross-legged wooden effigies of knights, probably 14th century. There is a memorial to Lady Wilbraham, d1705, rebuilder of the church, who c1671 set up within it a series of tablets to her ancestors in ornamental surrounds.

WETTON   *St Margaret*   SK 109554

The short but wide body of the church is of 1820, but the west tower with large quoins is 13th century with a 15th century upper stage.

Former chapel at Wheaton Aston

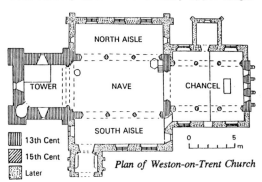

13th Cent
15th Cent
Later

Plan of Weston-on-Trent Church

Whitmore Church

Weston-on-Trent Church

WHEATON ASTON   *St Mary*   SJ 852125

A chapel existed here by 1318 and 14th century features are said to have survived at the east end until the total rebuilding of 1857 by Bidlake and Lovatt. A drawing of the church made in 1855 shows that until then most of its features, including two round arched windows with external shutters and a doorway reached by steps on the south side, and a tiny wooden belfry, dated from a rebuilding of 1770 which cost £400. A new chancel was added to a design by Charles Lynam in 1893.

WHITMORE   *St Mary and All Saints*   SJ 810410

Part of the nave walling on either side is Norman, but most of the rest dates from 1632 and 1676, and was restored in 1880. It forms a single body with a timber framed bellcote and square headed windows with round arched lights.

WHITTINGTON   *St Giles*   SK 158084

The west tower is probably 14th century with a later spire. There are small rooms on either side of it which are contemporary with the long nave of 1761 with Y-tracery in the windows. The southern room was extended in the 20th century, and a new chancel was built in 1881. The pulpit and tester are of 1671 and supposedly come from Lichfield Cathedral. There are fragments of medieval glass in the chancel windows. None of the many memorial tablets is on great age or much interest.

WOLSTANTON   *St Margaret*   SJ 857481

The church was entirely rebuilt in 1859-60, leaving only the 14th century north tower, the recumbent effigies of Sir William Sneyd, d1571, and his wife, and other memorials to William Sneyd, d1689, and John Sneyd, d1710.

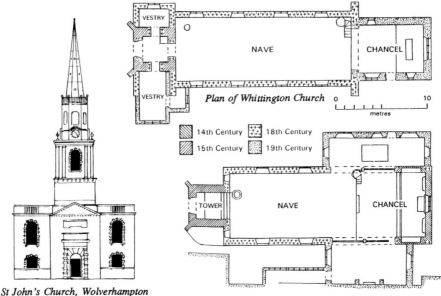

Plan of Whittington Church   0   10   metres

14th Century   18th Century
15th Century   19th Century

St John's Church, Wolverhampton

Plan of Weston-on-Trent Church

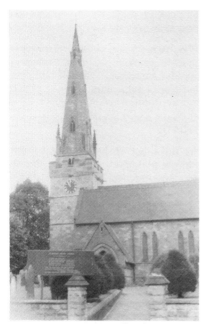

Wombourne Church

WOLVERHAMPTON   *St John*

SO 914982

This church of 1758-76 designed either by William Baker, or the mason Roger Eykyn, lies in a square beside the southern section of the ring road. It is entered below a fine west tower with an octagonal belfry and spire. There are two tiers of side windows, the topmost serving the galleries, and the east end has a blank Venetian window. The aisles have groin vaults and the main body has a segmental tunnel vault of plaster. The external ashlar was renewed in the 1980s.

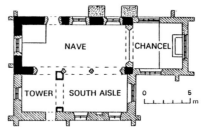

Plan of Wychnor Church

Font, St Peter's, Wolverhampton

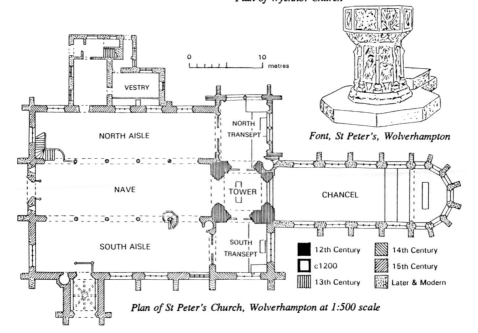

	12th Century		14th Century
	c1200		15th Century
	13th Century		Later & Modern

Plan of St Peter's Church, Wolverhampton at 1:500 scale

WOLVERHAMPTON   *St Peter*   SO 914988

The worn and grime-covered 9th century cross-shaft over 4m high in the churchyard near the south transept demonstrates the antiquity of this site as a place of worship. The shaft has pendant triangles and acanthus motifs. The church was collegiate in the medieval period and from 1479 to 1846 was classed as a "Royal Peculiar" united with St George's Chapel at Windsor Castle. As it stands now the church has been mostly refaced or rebuilt externally. There are extensive Victorian buttresses on the north side, and the chancel is of 1852-65 by Ewan Christian, replacing a shorter chancel in the Classical style built in 1682-4. The narrow late 13th century crossing arches below the tower contrast sharply with the wide and spacious nave and aisles of c1450-80 with five bays of arches on octagonal piers. The south transept with a fine five light east window is of c1300 with a late medieval clerestory, and there is a two storey south porch, now mostly Victorian. The north transept and the upper parts of the tower, both with extensive panelling, are early 16th century. As a result of alteration, probably in the late 17th century, the north transept windows now take an odd form with a mullion rising to a round head.

Built as one piece with one of the arcade piers is a splendid stone pulpit with much blank panelling, a lion guarding the base of the steps, and the arms of the Swynnerton family. The twelve chancel stalls were brought here from Lilleshall Abbey in Shropshire in 1546, whilst the lectern is said to be from Halesowen Abbey. In the south transept are alabaster effigies of John Leveson, d1575, and his wife, and a standing bronze effigy with two loose cherubs by Le Sueur to Admiral Sir Richard Leveson, d1605. In the north transept are alabaster effigies of Thomas Lane, d1585, and his wife, and a wall monument to Colonel John Lane, d1667.

WOMBOURNE   *St Benedict Biscop*   SO 876932

The dedication is said to be unique. The west tower and north side of the nave are 14th and 15th century but the rest of the church was rebuilt by Street in 1862-7. Within the church is a good small early 16th century Italian relief sculpture.

Saxon Cross, Wolverhampton

St Peter's Church, Wolverhampton

WYCHNOR   *St Leonard*   SK 177160

The 12th century nave was given a south aisle with a three bay arcade and a new chancel and chancel arch in the early 14th century. Soon afterwards the west bay of the aisle was made into a tower, an arch of c1200, perhaps the original chancel arch, being re-set beside the western arcade pier to support its east wall. The font is 15th century, and the brick upper stage of the tower is 16th 17th century. Only the east window and the two large buttresses on the north side are Victorian.

YOXALL   *St Peter*   SK 141190

Much of the church is of 1865-8 but the south doorway is a refaced piece of c1200, the five bay arcades are 14th century, the tower may be 17th century and has a old screen. There is an alabaster monument to Humphrey Welles, d1565, and his wife.

LIST OF LATER ANGLICAN CHURCHES

AMBLECOTE - Holy Trinity - 1841-4 by Samuel Heming.
AMINGTON - St Editha - 1864 by G.E.Street.
ASTON - St Saviour - 1846 by James Trubshaw, tower added 1870 by J.R.Botham.
BAGNALL - St Chad - 1834, chancel added in 1879-81 by J. Beardmore.
BALTERLEY - 1901 by Austin & Paley.
BASFORD - St Mark - 1914 by Austin & Paley.
BEDNALL - All Saints 1846 by H.Ward, tower added in 1873.
BENTLEY (Walsall) - Emmanuel - 1956 by Lavender, Twentyman & Percy.
BIDDULPH MOOR - 1863 by Ward & Ford.
BILSTON - St Luke - 1851-2 by Johnson & Son.
BILSTON - St Mary - 1827-9 by Goodwin.
BISHOPSWOOD - St John - 1851 by G.T.Robinson.
BLAKENALL HEATH (Walsall) - Christchurch - 1865-72 by Naden.
BLOXWICH - All Saints - c1791-4, much altered and extended in 1875-7.
BRADLEY (Wolverhampton) - St Martin - 1866-8 by Bidlake.
BRAMSHALL - St Lawrence - 1835 by Thomas Fradgley.
BRANSTON - St Saviour - 1864 by Street, enlarged in 1891.
BRERETON - St Michael - 1837 by T.Trubshaw, enlarged in 1877 by Sir G.G.Scott
BROCKMOOR - St John - 1844-5 by Thomas Smith.
BROWN EDGE - St Anne - 1844 by J.& C.Trubshaw, short tower added in 1854.
BROWNHILLS - St James- 1850-1 by G.T.Robinson.
BURNTWOOD - Christchurch - 1819-20 by Joseph Potter, north aisle added in 1869.
BURSLEM - St Paul - 1828-31 by Lewis Vulliamy.
BURTON-ON-TRENT - All Saints - 1903-5 by Naylor & Sale.
BURTON-ON-TRENT - Christchurch - 1843-4 by Joseph Mitchell
BURTON-ON-TRENT - Holy Trinity - 1823, entirely rebuilt 1880-2 by J. Oldrid Scott.
BURTON-ON-TRENT - St Aidan - 1884 by Giles & Brookhouse.
BURTON-ON-TRENT - St Chad - 1903-10 by Bodley.
BURTON-ON-TRENT - St John - 1864-6 by Edwin Holmes.
BURTON-ON-TRENT - St Margaret - 1881 by Reginald Churchill.
BURTON-ON-TRENT - St Mark - 1869 by Holmes.
BUTTERTON - St Thomas - 1844 by Thomas Hopper.
CALDMORE (Walsall) - St Michael - 1870-1 by J.R.Veall.
CANWELL - St Mary, St Giles & All Saints, 1911 by Temple Moore.
CHASETOWN - St Anne - 1865 by Edward Adams.
CHEADLE - St Giles - 1837-9 by J.P.Pritchett. Communion rail of 1687.
CHESTERTON - Holy Trinity - 1851-2 by H.Ward & Son.

COBRIDGE (Burslem) - Christchurch - 1838-40 by L.G.Hales.
COSELEY - Christchurch - 1829-30 by Thomas Lee.
COTES HEATH - 1837, chancel added by C.Lynam in 1891.
COTTON - St John - 1795.
COVEN - St Paul - 1857 by Banks.
CROXDEN - 1884-5 on site of chapel ante portas of Cistercian abbey.
CROXTON - St Paul - 1853-4 by Ewan Christian.
DARLASTON - All Saints - 1951-2 on site of church of 1871 bombed in WW2.
DARLASTON - St Lawrence - 1871-02 by A.P. Brevitt.
DENSTONE - All Saints - 1860-2 by Street.
DERRINGTON - St Matthew - c1845-7 by Henry Ward.
DUDLEY - St Augustine - 1884 by H.D.W.Drinkwater.
DUDLEY - St James - 1840.
DUDLEY - St John - 1840.
DUDLEY - St Thomas - 1815-18 by William Brooks.
DUDLEY WOOD - St John - 1931 by Sir Charles Nicholson.
DUNSTALL - St Mary - 1852-3 by Henry Clutton.
EDINGALE - Holy Trinity - 1880-1 by C.Lynam.
ELKSTONE - St John the Baptist - 1786-8.
ESSINGTON - St John - 1932-3 by Wood & Kendrick.
ETTINGSHALL (Wolverhampton) - St Martin - 1938 by Lavender & Twentyman.
ETRURIA - St Matthew - 1848-9 by H.Ward & Son.
FAZELEY - St Paul - 1853-5 - by H.J.Stevens.
FENTON - Christchurch - 1890-1 by Charles Lynan, tower added 1899.
FENTON - St Michael - 1887 by Lewis & Son.
FLASH - St Paul - 1901 by W.R.Bryden.
FORSBROOK - St Peter - 1848-9 by James & Edward Barr. North aisle 1912.
FOXT - 1838.
FRADLEY - 1861 by T.W.Goodman.
FREEHAY - St Chad - 1842-3 by Scott & Moffatt.
FULFORD - St Nicholas - 1825 by C.H.Winks.
FULLBROOK (Walsall) - St Gabriel - 1939 by Lavender & Twentyman.
GAILEY - Christchurch - 1849-51 by G.T.Robinson, chancel 1875 by J. Fowler.
GENTLESHAW - Christchurch - 1839, east end added in 1903.
GLASCOTE - St George - 1880 by Basil Champneys.
GOLDENHILL (Tunstall) - St John - 1840-1 by Stanley.
GREAT BARR - St Margaret - 1860-1 by Griffin.
GREAT WYRLEY - St Mark - 1844-5 by T.Johnson.
GREEN HEATH - St Saviour - 1887-8 by F.W.Evans, chancel of 1901.
GREETS GREEN (West Bromwich) - St Peter - 1857-8 by T.Johnson & Son.
HALES - St Mary - 1856 by George Gilbert Scott.
HAMMERWICH - St John the Baptist - 1873-83 by Newman & Billing.
HANFORD - St Matthias - 1862 by Rushworth, and 1868 by Charles Lynam.
HANLEY - All Saints - 1910-13 by Gerald Horsley.
HANLEY - Holy Trinity - 1848-9 by J. Trubshaw.
HANLEY - St Jude - 1898-1901 by R.Scrivenor & Son.
HANLEY - St Luke - 1852-4 by H.Ward & Son.
HANLEY - St Mark - 1831-3 by J. Oates, chancel added by Scrivenor in 1868.
HAYWOOD - St Stephen - 1840 by Thomas Trubshaw.
HEATH HAYES - St John - 1902-3 by F.T.Beck.
HEATH TOWN (Wolverhampton) - Holy Trinity - 1850-2 by E.Banks.
HEDNESFORD - St Peter - 1868 by T.H. Rushworth.
HILDERSTONE - Christchurch - 1827-9 by Thomas Trubshaw.

HINTS - St Bartholomew - 1882-3 by John Oldrid Scott. Older monuments.
HIXON - St Peter - c1845-8 by George Gilbert Scott.
HOAR CROSS - Holy Angels - 1872-6 by Bodley, various later additions.
HOLLINGTON - St John - 1859-61 by Street.
HOLLINSCLOUGH - St Agnes - 1840. House adjoins to west.
HOPWAS - St Chad - 1881 by John Douglas.
HURST HILL - St Mary - 1872 by G. Bidlake, chancel added in 1882 by Fleeming.
KIDSGROVE - 1837 probaby by Mrs Kinnersley of Clough Hall.
KINGSTONE - St John - 1860-1 by David Brandon.
KNIGHTLEY - Christchurch - 1840-1 by Thomas Trubshaw.
KNUTTON - St Mary - 1872-4 by T.Lewis & Son.
LEEK - All Saints - 1885-7 by Norman Shaw.
LEEK - St Luke - 1847-8 by F.&.H.Francis.
LITTLE ASTON - St Peter - 1873-4 by Street.
LONGSDON - St Chad - 1903-5 by Gerald Horsley.
LONGTON - Holy Evangelists - 1847 by G.G.Scott, north aisle added 1891-2.
LONGTON - Holy Trinity - 1890-1.
LONGTON - Resurrection - 1853, enlarged in 1873 and 1903.
LONGTON - St James the Less - 1832-4 by T.Trubshaw.
LONGTON - St Mary & St Chad, 1898 by J.M.Brooks, baptistry added in 1910.
LOWER GORNAL - St James - 1815-23, enlarged in 1836 by E.March, altered 1863.
MARCHINGTON WOODLANDS - St John - 1858-9 by A.D.Gough.
MEERBROOK - St Matthew - 1868 & 1873 by Norman Shaw. Chapel of 1565 gone.
MILTON - St Philip & St James - 1865, extended at west end c1970.
MODDERSHALL - All Saints - 1903.
MORETON - All Saints - 1837-8.
MOW COP - St Thomas - 1841-2 by T. Stanley.
MOXLEY - 1850-1 by W.Horton.
NEEDWOOD FOREST - Christchurch - 1809, altered in 1880.
NETHERTON - St Andrew - 1827-30 by Thomas Lee.
NEWBOROUGH - All Saints - 1899-1901 by J.Oldrid Scott.
NEWCASTLE-UNDER-LYME - St George - 1828 by Bedford.
NEWCASTLE-UNDER-LYME - St Paul - 1905-8 by R. Scrivener & Son.
NEWCHAPEL - St James - 1878-80 by T.Lewis & Son.
NEWTOWN - 1837.
NORTON CANES - St James - 1832, rebuilt in 1888 by Osborn & Reading.
OAKAMOOR - Holy Trinity - 1832 by J.P.Pritchett.
OCKER HILL (West Bromwich) - St Mark - 1849 by Hamilton & Saunders.
OULTON - St John -1874 by R. Scrivener & Son.
PALFREY (Walsall) - St Mary & All Saints - 1901-2 by J.E.K & J.P.Cutts.
PELSALL - St Michael - 1843-4 by George E. Hamilton.
PENKHULL (Stoke) - St Thomas, 1843 by Scott & Moffatt, with aisles of 1892.
PENSNETT - St Mark - 1846-9 by J.M.Derick.
PORT HILL (Wolstanton) - St Andrew - 1886 by A.R.Wood, south aisle added 1897.
QUARRY BANK - Christchurch - 1845-6 by Thomas Smith, chancel of 1900.
RANGEMORE - All Saints - 1866-7 by Butterfield, aisle 1884, chancel 1895.
REAPS MOOR - St John 1842. House attached. Former school room below church.
SALT - St James - 1840-2 by Thomas Trubshaw.
SEDGLEY - All Saints - 1826-9 by Thomas Lee.
SHORT HEATH - Holy Trinity - 1854-5 by W.Horton.
SILVERDALE - St Luke - 1853 by R. Armstrong.
SLINDON - St Chad - 1894 by Basil Champneys.
STAFFORD - St John - 1928 by Sir Charles Nicholson. Nave not built.
STAFFORD - St Paul - 1844 by Henry Ward

STAFFORD - St Thomas - 1862-4 by W.Culshaw.
STANTON - St Mary - 1846-7 by W. Evans.
STOKE-ON-TRENT - All Saints - 1887-8 by Lynam & Rickman.
STOKE-ON-TRENT - Holy Trinity 1842 by George Gilbert Scott.
STONE - Christchurch - 1885, with a nave added 1899 by CharlesLynam.
STONNALL - St Peter - 1822, chancel added by Joseph Potter in 1843.
STRAMSHALL - St Michael - 1850-2 by Thomas Fradgley.
STRETTON (nr Burton) - St Mary - 1895-7 by Micklethwaite & Somers Clarke.
TALKE - St Martin -1794, bell turret and transept added c1850.
TALKE - St Saviour - 1879 by F.W.Hunt. Demolished in 1971.
TETTENHALL - Christchurch - 1865-6 by Bateman & Corser.
TIPTON - St Martin - 1795-7 by J. Keyte, extended at either end in 1874-6.
TIPTON - St Matthew - 1876 by J.H.Gibbons.
TIPTON - St Paul - 1837-8 by Robert Ebbles.
TIXALL - St John - 1849 by Wyatt & Brandon.
TRENT VALE (Stoke) - St John - 1909. South nave of church of 1843-5.
TUNSTALL - Christchurch - 1830-1 by F.Bedford.
TUNSTALL - St Mary - 1858-9 by J.W. & J.Hay
UPPER GORNAL - St Peter - 1840-1 by R. Ebbles.
UPPER TEAN - Christchurch - 1843 by Johnson.
WALL - St John - c1840-3 probably by Scott & Moffatt.
WALSALL - St Andrew - 1884-7 by J.E.K.Cutts.
WALSALL - St John - 1857-8 by Griffin & Weller
WALSALL - St Mark - 1871.
WALSALL - St Paul - 1891-3 by Pearson.
WALSALL - St Peter - 1841 by Isaac Highway.
WALSALL WOOD - St John - 1837 by Highway, south aisle and chancel 1895.
WALTON-ON-THE-HILL - St Thomas - 1842 by Thomas Trubshaw.
WARSLOW - St Laurence - 1820, chancel added by Lynam & Sons in 1908.
WEDNESBURY - St James - 1847-8 by W.Horton, chancel added 1857, apse 1865.
WEDNESBURY - St John - 1845-6 by Dawkes & Hamilton.
WEST BROMWICH - Annunciation - 1956-8 by Hickton, Madeley & S.T. Salt
WEST BROMWICH - Christchurch - 1821-9 by Francis Goodwin
WEST BROMWICH - Good Shepherd with St John - 1967-8 by John Madin.
WEST BROMWICH - Holy Trinity - 1840-1 by J.W.Dawkes.
WEST BROMWICH - St James - 1839-41 by Ebbles, SW tower added c1890.
WETLEY ROCKS - St John - 1833-4, chancel added in 1901 by J.Beardmore.
WHISTON - St Mildred - 1910 by J.H.Beckett.
WIGGINTON - St Leonard - 1777, chancel added by Joyce in 1861-2.
WILLENHALL - St Anne - 1856-8 by H. Jeavons.
WILLENHALL - St Giles - 1866-7 by W.D.Griffin.
WILLENHALL - St Stephen - 1853-4 by Griffin.
WILNECOTE - Holy Trinity - 1821.
WOLVERHAMPTON - All Saints - 1877-9 by Smith & Roper, chancel added 1892-3.
WOLVERHAMPTON - Christchurch - 1867 by E. Banks.
WOLVERHAMPTON - St Andrew - 1965-7 by Twentyman, Percy & Partners
WOLVERHAMPTON - St Barnabas - 1892-3 by T.H.Fleeming.
WOLVERHAMPTON - St Chad - 1907-8 by F.T.Beck.
WOLVERHAMPTON - St George - 1828-30 by James Morgan. Now a supermarket.
WOLVERHAMPTON - St Jude - 1867-9 by Bidlake.
WOLVERHAMPTON - St Luke - 1860-1 by G.T.Robinson.
WOLVERHAMPTON - St Mark - 1848-9 by C.W.Orford.
WOLVERHAMPTON - St Stephen - 1907-9 by F.T.Beck.
WORDSLEY - Holy Trinity - 1829-30 by Lewis Vulliamy. East window of 1857.

GLOSSARY OF ARCHITECTURAL TERMS

Apse	- Semi-circular or polygonal east end of a church containing an altar.
Ashlar	- Masonry of blocks with even faces and square edges.
Ballflower	- Globular flower of three petals enclosing ball. Current c1310-40.
Baroque	- A whimsical and odd form of the Classical architectural style.
Beakhead	- Decorative motif of bird or beast heads, often biting a roll moulding.
Broaches	- Sloping half pyramids adapting an octagonal spire to a square tower.
Chancel	- The eastern part of a church used by the clergy.
Chevron Ornament	- A Norman ornament with continuous Vs forming a zig-zag.
Clerestory	- An upper storey pierced by windows lighting the floor below.
Coffering	- Sunk square or polygonal panels on a ceiling.
Collar Beam	- A tie-beam used higher up near the apex of the roof.
Crossing Tower	- A tower built on four arches in the middle of a cruciform church.
Cruciform Church	- A cross-shaped church with transepts forming the arms of the cross.
Cusp	- A projecting point between the foils of a foiled Gothic arch.
Dado	- The decorative covering of the lower part of a wall or screen.
Dog Tooth	- Four centered stars placed diagonally and raised pyramidally.
Easter Sepulchre	- A recess in a chancel which received an effigy of Christ at Easter.
Elizabethan	- Of the time of Queen Elizabeth I (1558-1603).
Fan Vault	- Vault with fan-like patterns. In fashion from c1440 to 1530.
Foil	- A lobe formed by the cusping of a circle or arch.
Four Centred Arch	- A low, flattish arch with each curve drawn from two compass points.
Head Stops	- Heads of humans or beasts forming the ends of a hoodmould.
Hoodmould	- A projecting moulding above a lintel or arch to throw off water.
Impost	- A wall bracket, often moulded, to support the end of an arch.
Jacobean	- Of the time of King James I (1603-25).
Jamb	- The side of a doorway, window, or other opening.
King Post	- An upright timber connecting a tie-beam with a collar-beam.
Lancet	- A long and comparatively narrow window with a pointed head.
Light	- A compartment of a window.
Lintel	- A horizontal stone or beam spanning an opening.
Low-side window	- A window with a low sill allowing those outside a chancel to see inside.
Miserichord	- Bracket underneath hinged choir stall seat to support standing person.
Mullion	- A vertical member dividing the lights of a window.
Nave	- The part of a church in which the congregation sits or stands.
Norman	- A division of English Romanesque architecture from 1066 to 1200.
Ogival Arch	- Arch of oriental origin with both convex and concave curves.
Pilaster	- Flat buttress or pier attached to a wall.
Piscina	- A stone basin used for rinsing out holy vessels after a mass.
Plinth	- The projecting base of a wall.
Queen Posts	- Two vertical timbers connecting a tie-beam and a collar-beam.
Quoins	- Dressed stones at the corners of a building.
Respond	- A half pier or column bonded into a wall and carrying an arch.
Reticulation	- Tracery with a net-like appearence. Current c1330-70.
Rococo	- The late phase of the Baroque style, current in mid 18th century.
Rood Screen	- A screen with a crucifix mounted on it between a nave and chancel.
Sedilia	- Seats for clergy (usually three) in the south wall of a chancel.
Spandrel	- The surface between two arches.
Tester	- A sounding board above a 17th or 18th century pulpit.
Tie-Beam	- A beam connecting the slopes of a roof at or near its foot.
Tracery	- Intersecting ribwork in the upper part of a later Gothic window.
Transom	- A horizontal member dividing the lights of a window.
Triptych	- Three surfaces, usually sculpted or painted, joined by hinges.
Tuscan	- An order of Classical architecture.
Tympanum	- The space between the lintel of a doorway and the arch above it.
Venetian Window	- Window with a square headed light on either side of an arched light.
Volute	- Spiral scroll used as a componant of an Ionic column.